Cambrid

Shakesp

The Tempest

Rex Gibson

Series Editor: Rex Gibson

CAMBRIDGE
UNIVERSITY PRESS

CAMBRIDGE UNIVERSITY PRESS
Cambridge, New York, Melbourne, Madrid, Cape Town, Singapore, São Paulo

Cambridge University Press
The Edinburgh Building, Cambridge CB2 2RU, UK

www.cambridge.org
Information on this title: www.cambridge.org/9780521538572

© Cambridge University Press 2004

First published 2004
Reprinted 2006

Printed in the United Kingdom at the University Press, Cambridge

A catalogue record for this publication is available from the British Library

ISBN-13 978-0-521-53857-2 paperback
ISBN-10 0-521-53857-2 paperback

Cover image: © Getty Images/PhotoDisc

Contents

Introduction

The Tempest lends itself to many different kinds of interpretation. It can be thought of simply as a story. Before the play begins, Prospero, Duke of Milan, has been overthrown by his brother, Antonio, aided by King Alonso of Naples and the king's brother, Sebastian. Prospero and his daughter Miranda have been exiled to an island, where, over a period of 12 years, he has perfected his magic and made Caliban, the only other human inhabitant of the island, his slave. The play tells how Prospero raises a tempest that shipwrecks his enemies on the island, where he subjects them to ordeals, but finally forgives them.

Alternatively, the title, *The Tempest*, can be interpreted symbolically: representing the emotional and spiritual turmoil suffered by the characters. In yet another approach, *The Tempest* can be understood through its themes. Here the play is viewed as Shakespeare's dramatic exploration of issues important to his times (and ours): rightful authority, forgiveness rather than revenge, colonialism (particularly the European exploitation of the peoples of the Americas), nature versus nurture, imprisonment and freedom, magic, sleep and dreams.

The Tempest can also be thought of as a particular type of play which Shakespeare wrote towards the end of his career. It is the last in a group of four, often called the 'late plays'. The others are *Pericles*, *Cymbeline* and *The Winter's Tale*. They are romances, portraying dangers, misfortunes and separations, but ending happily. Romance stories contain all kinds of fairytale improbabilities, mixing together love, storms, feasts, and journeys to faraway places where magical events occur. They tell of loss and recovery, of royal children thought to be dead, but like Ferdinand, found to be living.

However you choose to approach *The Tempest*, its enigmatic, ambiguous features are striking. Things are not what they seem. The play begins with an illusion: the shipwreck is an act of Prospero's magic. What seems so disastrously real is only a fiction. That sense of illusion characterises the island and its original inhabitants, the airy spirit Ariel and the earthy Caliban. The haunting music and the ever-present echoes of the sea add to the sense of wonder and mystery that pervades the island. But above all, *The Tempest* is a play: an invitation to the imagination to bring the text to dramatic life.

Commentary

Act 1 Scene 1

In what is surely the most dramatic opening scene in any of his plays, Shakespeare sets every director of *The Tempest* a fearsomely challenging task: how to stage the storm and shipwreck? Shakespeare's first stage direction makes the demand evident:

> *A tempestuous noise of thunder and lightning. Enter a SHIPMASTER, a BOATSWAIN and MARINERS*

The scene takes place on a ship at sea during a terrible storm. Just how can the fury of the waves and wind be shown on stage? How can the actors ensure that the dialogue, with its remarkably accurate nautical commands by the Boatswain, be heard above the noise of the thunder? Some productions use elaborate sets to create the impression of a realistic ship foundering in a gale. Others play the scene on a bare stage without props or scenery, using only lighting, sound effects and actors' movements to create the illusion of a ship caught in a tempest.

The Master orders the Boatswain to save the ship from running aground, but the entry of King Alonso and the courtiers hinders the Boatswain's work. In the Boatswain's angry response, Shakespeare immediately raises an issue that will run through the whole play: who possesses rightful authority? Although the sailor is of far lower status than the king and the noblemen, he peremptorily orders them to return to their cabins:

> Hence! What cares these roarers for the name of king? To
> cabin. Silence! Trouble us not.   *(lines 15–16)*

On land, such blunt speaking would result in swift punishment for insolence. Here, on a crisis-stricken ship, the Boatswain's authority exceeds the king's and, after more plain speaking about the courtiers' powerlessness in the face of the storm, the Boatswain's curt order is obeyed: 'Out of our way, I say.' The king and courtiers leave, with Gonzalo drawing comfort from his claim that the Boatswain looks like a man born to be hanged rather than drowned: 'his complexion is perfect gallows'. But as the Boatswain continues to issue orders to the mariners, Sebastian and Antonio return, and their vicious natures, which will become all too clear as the play unfolds, are revealed as they curse the Boatswain:

SEBASTIAN A pox o'your throat, you bawling, blasphemous,
    incharitable dog.
BOATSWAIN Work you then.
ANTONIO Hang, cur, hang, you whoreson, insolent noisemaker
(lines 36–9)

The Boatswain orders action to save the ship, but disaster strikes and the Boatswain takes comfort in drink: 'What, must our mouths be cold?' As Antonio once again curses the Boatswain, the crew abandon hope, each sailor facing death in a different way. Some pray or beg for God's mercy, others bid farewell to each other or to their wives and children. As the vessel splits, Antonio and Sebastian resolve to join King Alonso below. Gonzalo accepts whatever is to come, but wishes for death on dry land:

> Now would I give a thousand furlongs of sea for an acre of barren ground – long heath, brown furze, anything. The wills above be done, but I would fain die a dry death.
(lines 58–60)

Act 1 Scene 2

This long scene (500 lines) contains a number of distinct but linked episodes:

- Prospero's story, lines 1–186: The tempest is revealed to be caused by Prospero's 'art' (magic) in order to bring his enemies within his power. He tells his story of how he was overthrown as Duke of Milan, cast adrift on the ocean, and arrived at the island.
- Ariel's story, lines 187–305: Ariel tells how he obeyed Prospero's orders to shipwreck the vessel. Prospero reminds Ariel of how he freed him from imprisonment by Sycorax.
- Caliban's story, lines 306–74: Caliban describes how Prospero enslaved him after he had made Prospero welcome to the island.

- Ferdinand and Miranda, lines 375–500: Ferdinand grieves for his father, King Alonso, believing him to be drowned. He and Miranda fall in love, but Prospero treats him harshly.

Scene 2 opens with Miranda begging her father Prospero to calm the tempest. She is full of pity for the suffering of the shipwrecked people, but Prospero assures her that no one is hurt, 'Tell your piteous heart / There's no harm done.' Inviting Miranda to help him remove his 'magic garment', which gives him the supernatural powers that he calls his 'art', he reveals that the shipwreck was an illusion his magic has created, and the passengers and crew are all safe. Some productions begin the scene by showing Prospero as a powerful magician, his arms raised as he calms the storm at Miranda's request. Other productions begin the scene quietly, after the storm has ended, providing a marked contrast to the frenzied activity of Scene 1.

Prospero decides 'The hour's now come' when he must tell Miranda her life story and reveal why he has caused the tempest that seems to have wrecked the vessel. He questions her about what she remembers before they came to 'this cell', the island cave in which they now live. Although she was only three years old (she is now fifteen), she recalls, almost as a dream, that she once had four or five women attendants. Prospero confirms her recollection ('Thou hadst, and more') and demands, in a striking image of a long distant past:

> What seest thou else
> In the dark backward and abysm of time?   *(lines 49–50)*

Miranda can remember nothing else, so Prospero embarks on the story of how they came to the island. It seems significant that Shakespeare begins Propcro's tale by having him briefly display a sense of humour that will be seen only rarely throughout the play:

PROSPERO Twelve year since, Miranda, twelve year since,
    Thy father was the Duke of Milan and
    A prince of power –
MIRANDA   Sir, are not you my father?
PROSPERO Thy mother was a piece of virtue, and
    She said thou wast my daughter   *(lines 53–7)*

Prospero tells of the 'foul play' that ejected him and his daughter from Milan, and of the blessed help that brought them to the island. He describes how he was once the unchallenged ruler of the most important state in Italy, 'Through all the signories [Italian states] it was the first, / And Prospero the prime duke'. But because of his overwhelming interest in acquiring magical skills, Prospero entrusted the government of Milan to Antonio, his brother, and 'to my state grew stranger, being transported / And rapt in secret studies'.

His total neglect of state affairs brought about his downfall. Antonio proved to be false. To serve his own interests, Antonio learned whom to promote, and whom to cut down to size ('who t'advance, and who / To trash for over-topping'). He won the loyalty of Prospero's followers, and, possessing both the officials and position ('officer, and office'), was able to make everyone in Milan dance to his tune. Like a parasitic ivy which destroys the tree it grows on, he took over all of Prospero's power to rule. These two images of music and of parasitic ivy are vividly expressed:

> set all hearts i'th'state
> To what tune pleased his ear, that now he was
> The ivy which had hid my princely trunk,
> And sucked my verdure out on't   *(lines 84–7)*

Prospero's angry feelings as he tells of his scheming brother are conveyed in the confused syntax of his speech, but his agitation seems to spill over and causes him to rebuke Miranda for not listening, '– thou attend'st not!' His reprimand raises questions about his relationship with his daughter. Some actors have portrayed Prospero as a strict and emotionally inhibited parent; but other, more lovingly tender interpretations have been performed. Prospero continues his tale of how his preference for study and neglect of his duties aroused his brother's evil nature. Prospero's trust was betrayed as Antonio abused the wealth and power he acquired and, 'his ambition growing', plotted to become the part he played: the duke himself, 'Absolute Milan'.

Antonio saw Prospero's absorption with study as showing he was unfit to govern. Consumed by his passion for power ('So dry he was for sway'), Antonio made a treaty with Alonso the king of Naples, Prospero's long-standing enemy. The agreement was that in exchange for ('in lieu o'th'premises') making Milan subordinate to Naples, and for protection money ('tribute'), Alonso would overthrow Prospero and make Antonio Duke of Milan. The theme of rightful authority is once again evident, just as it was made clear in Scene 1 in the exchanges between the Boatswain and the courtiers. But here the deceitful nature of the illegal seizure of power is highlighted in Antonio's treachery: under cover of darkness he would open the gates of Milan to give Alonso's army the opportunity to enter the city and capture Prospero and Miranda.

Because of the great love the people of Milan felt for Prospero, the conspirators did not dare to kill him. Instead, they cast him and his infant daughter adrift in a tiny, unseaworthy boat. Prospero's description of the boat and of their ordeal is poignantly balanced by his witness to nature's pity and kindness ('th'winds, whose pity sighing back again / Did us but loving wrong') and of the comfort and strength to endure that he drew from Miranda's presence: he describes her as 'a cherubin' who preserved him.

Prospero continues to catalogue the good fortune he and Miranda experienced in their affliction. They were brought to the island by the help of the gods ('providence divine'), and the kindly Gonzalo had given much practical help in storing the boat with food, water and clothes, and with Prospero's beloved books, 'volumes that / I prize above my dukedom'. There is a benign dramatic irony in Miranda's wish that she might see Gonzalo ('Would I might / But ever see that man'), and some actors playing Prospero acknowledge it with a quiet smile, knowing that his magic will soon result in Miranda's wish being fulfilled. But Prospero now quickly concludes his story of their 'sea-sorrow'. Since arriving on the island he has tutored Miranda, and he has just caused the tempest because 'bountiful Fortune', his 'dear lady', has delivered his enemies into his hands. His fortunes now stand at their 'zenith' (highest point), and he must take action to ensure their success.

Prospero's long story of his usurpation and exile is now ended. He magically causes Miranda to sleep, and calls for Ariel. Ariel is an 'airy spirit' who describes his powers and his relationship to Prospero in his opening words:

> All hail, great master, grave sir, hail! I come
> To answer thy best pleasure; be't to fly,

> To swim, to dive into the fire, to ride
> On the curled clouds. To thy strong bidding task
> Ariel, and all his quality.   *(lines 189–93)*

Ariel reports that he has carried out Prospero's commands in exact detail. His miraculous display of fire caused terror on the ship. His description of how he 'flamed amazement' all over the vessel resembles the strange effect of light called Saint Elmo's fire, well known to sailors caught in storms at sea. Shakespeare's imagination may have been stirred by a letter written by William Strachey in 1610, which told of such fantastic lightning seen during a shipwreck off Bermuda (see page 66). Ariel's actions seemed to drive everyone mad, and the passengers leapt overboard. First to jump was the king's son Ferdinand with the frantic cry, 'Hell is empty, / And all the devils are here'.

Ariel tells that the passengers are now safe on shore, and the sailors asleep aboard the ship, securely in harbour in a secret bay ('deep nook') of the island. The rest of the fleet is returning sadly home to Naples, mourning the loss of King Alonso in the shipwreck. Prospero is pleased with Ariel's performance, but his reminder that 'there's more work' provokes a protest from the spirit, 'Is there more toil?' In traditional tales, the spirits who served magicians were often resentful, and Ariel is no exception. His defiance of Prospero as he demands his liberty is yet another instance of the theme of challenges to authority which sounds through the play. Prospero is angered by what he sees as his servant's insubordination, labelling it resentment ('think'st it much') at the difficult and miraculous tasks Ariel has performed for him:

> to tread the ooze
> Of the salt deep,
> To run upon the sharp wind of the north,
> To do me business in the veins o'th'earth
> When it is baked with frost.   *(lines 252–6)*

Prospero reminds the aggrieved Ariel of how he freed him from Sycorax. The story he tells deepens the atmosphere of mystery that characterises the island. Sycorax, a 'foul witch', had so enraged the inhabitants of Algiers with her many wrongdoings and evil spells ('mischiefs manifold, and sorceries terrible / To enter human hearing') that they had banished her from the city. She was exiled to the island where she enslaved Ariel. His refusal to carry out her obscene and hateful commands enraged her utterly, so she imprisoned him inside a tree for twelve years. During that time she died, leaving the island inhabited only by Caliban, the son born to her there, and by the grievously suffering Ariel. Prospero, arriving on the island, used his magic to split the imprisoning pine tree and free Ariel. But Prospero displays the harsh side of his nature as he threatens Ariel with similar dire punishment if he continues to protest:

> If thou more murmur'st, I will rend an oak
> And peg thee in his knotty entrails till
> Thou hast howled away twelve winters.   *(lines 294–6)*

The threat prompts Ariel to beg for pardon. Stage performances have portrayed very different ways in which he submits and agrees to 'do my spiriting gently'. Some Ariels have appeared genuinely humble and contrite, but others have made it clear that their request for pardon is insincere, and their resentment remains as strong as ever (see page 61 for a striking example). Prospero seems satisfied and promises Ariel freedom. He instructs the spirit to disguise himself as an invisible sea-nymph and then return. With Ariel's departure the next episode in the scene begins as Prospero wakes Miranda and proposes to visit Caliban. His description of Caliban's services, making fire, bringing in wood and other 'offices / That profit us', suggests much about their relationship, as does his call for Caliban to appear:

> What ho! Slave! Caliban!
> Thou earth, thou! Speak!   *(lines 314–15)*

Caliban grumbles from off stage, 'There's wood enough within', but Prospero insists on his entry, calling him 'tortoise' as criticism of his slowness. After giving secret instructions to Ariel, newly appeared '*like a water-nymph*', Prospero once again insultingly commands Caliban:

> Thou poisonous slave, got by the devil himself
> Upon thy wicked dam, come forth.   *(lines 320–1)*

Caliban enters and curses Prospero and Miranda. In reply, Prospero promises to afflict him with all kinds of pains: 'cramps', 'Side-stitches' and pinches more painful than bee-stings. The source of Caliban's animosity is made plain in the story he now tells, which once again expresses the theme of rightful authority, here in the clear-cut question of who rightly owns the island:

> This island's mine by Sycorax my mother,
> Which thou tak'st from me. *(lines 332–3)*

Caliban recalls how Prospero had treated him kindly when he first arrived on the island, and that in return he had loved Prospero and shown him 'all the qualities o'th'isle'. But Prospero had enslaved him and taken possession of the island, keeping him like a pig in captivity ('sty me / In this hard rock'). Prospero angrily explains his motive: he had treated Caliban humanely, even taking him into his own cell, but Caliban had attempted to rape Miranda. Caliban's retort, that he wished he had succeeded in the rape and so populated the island with his children, provokes an impassioned denunciation by Miranda. She tells him he deserves his enslavement because he and his kind are naturally evil, capable only of vile acts. Her claim that she taught Caliban to speak evokes his contemptuous response:

> You taught me language, and my profit on't
> Is, I know how to curse. The red plague rid you
> For learning me your language! *(lines 363–5)*

The exchanges between Caliban and Prospero and Miranda have been much argued over as to the reality that lies behind them. Some have claimed that Caliban was an innocent, naturally good person, whose genuine friendship for Miranda was wrongly interpreted as intent to rape. Others have asserted that he was indeed a savage brute, tamed by Prospero, but whose true nature came out in the rape attempt. Yet other interpretations focus on Prospero. Some see him as a sincere and kind person who had no intention of seizing the island until Caliban's evil nature was revealed. Others argue for his greediness and deceit, determined from the outset to exploit the island's natural resources for his own profit, and always intending to enslave Caliban. You can find more on the background to these competing interpretations on pages 72–5 and 96–9.

There is a further much discussed puzzle relating to Miranda's outburst against Caliban ('Abhorrèd slave . . .', lines 351–62). Although in the Folio (see page 64) the lines are spoken by Miranda, throughout much of the eighteenth and nineteenth century, in both stage productions and in printed editions of the play, the lines were given to Prospero. Many critics and audience members felt that such harsh words were out of character for Miranda.

The episode ends with yet more curses, orders and threats of punishment by Prospero. Caliban leaves, acknowledging Prospero's superior power, even over Sycorax's god, Setebos. Caliban's departure is the cue for the final episode in Scene 2, which concerns Ferdinand. After the angry exchanges of Caliban and Prospero, the change in mood is marked, becoming one of quiet harmony. In many productions Ferdinand enters, led by the 'invisible' Ariel, and is clearly amazed and entranced by the sweet music that Ariel plays and sings. The song is about the calming of the tempest, an invitation to dance by the seashore, where the waves become silent and calm:

> Come unto these yellow sands,
> And then take hands.
> Curtsied when you have, and kissed,
> The wild waves whist. *(lines 375–8)*

Ariel invites the spirits to join in the chorus of watch-dogs barking and cockerels crowing. Ferdinand, much moved, says that the music calms both the storm and his feeling of grief for his father whom he believes drowned. Ariel's second song, 'Full fathom five thy father lies', appears to be directly addressed to Ferdinand, to comfort him. It tells how Alonso is magically transformed: his bones into coral, his eyes into pearl. The song seems intended to reassure the grieving son, telling him to think of his father not as dead, but as having undergone

> a sea-change
> Into something rich and strange. *(lines 400–1)*

Prospero's intention in causing the shipwreck is not only to bring his enemies within his power, but also to engineer the meeting of

Miranda and Ferdinand. As the scene develops, it is clear that whatever his outward behaviour, he hopes they will fall in love. His elaborately expressed command to Miranda, 'The fringèd curtains of thine eye advance, / And say what thou seest yond', may be Shakespeare's way of indicating that what follows is part of the artificial tradition of Romance, that the two young people will fall in love at first sight. And sure enough they do. Miranda's first thought is that Ferdinand is a spirit, but after Prospero's assurance that he is indeed human, she makes her admiration evident:

> I might call him
> A thing divine, for nothing natural
> I ever saw so noble. *(lines 416–18)*

Ferdinand is equally overwhelmed by the sight of Miranda: 'Most sure the goddess / On whom these airs attend.' Addressing her as 'O you wonder', he asks if she is a maid. Hearing her reply, 'No wonder, sir, / But certainly a maid', Ferdinand is amazed to hear his own language spoken, but his statement that he is 'the best of them that speak this speech' provokes a sharp response from Prospero, who demands to know what the king of Naples would think of such a claim. Ferdinand, believing his father dead, replies that he is king of Naples. Miranda's pity makes her love for Ferdinand evident, and he displays equal affection for her, vowing to make her queen of Naples. Prospero is secretly pleased that the two young people have fallen in love as he planned, but he puts on a stern appearance to test their love. In yet another example of the play's concern with the theme of rightful authority, Prospero accuses Ferdinand of intending to steal both the throne of Naples and the island:

> Thou dost here usurp
> The name thou ow'st not, and hast put thyself
> Upon this island as a spy, to win it
> From me, the lord on't. *(lines 452–5)*

Ferdinand denies the accusation of usurpation, and Miranda defends him, claiming that his handsome looks reflect his virtuous character: 'There's nothing ill can dwell in such a temple.' In all his plays, Shakespeare explores the disjunction between appearance and reality, showing that outward beauty can conceal inward evil. It appears that he is meaning to emphasise here the innocence and naivety of Miranda. Prospero is unimpressed by Ferdinand's denial and Miranda's plea. He calls Ferdinand a traitor and threatens harsh punishments. Ferdinand tries to resist and draws his sword, but Prospero magically 'freezes' him and makes him drop the weapon. Miranda again pleads for Ferdinand, stressing his gentility and good intentions, but Prospero rebukes her for daring to teach him wisdom, 'What, I say, / My foot my tutor?' He also scolds Miranda as a 'Foolish wench' who cannot see that Ferdinand is just like Caliban.

Prospero seems determined to punish Ferdinand, who is still weak from the spell cast upon him. Ferdinand declares he is content to accept all the afflictions he suffers: his father's death, his weakness, the shipwreck and any threat Prospero might carry out. He can endure all these as long as he has the chance, once a day, to see Miranda from the confines of his prison. The whole episode of Ferdinand echoes two elements of the 'Romance tradition', which probably partly influenced Shakespeare as he wrote *The Tempest* (see page 69): first, the harsh father who submits a young lover to ordeals and trials in order to test his love; second, the power of love to overcome all suffering. Ferdinand's devotion to Miranda, hoping to glimpse her daily as he undergoes hardship, strongly suggests this fairytale world in which love conquers all.

Prospero, outwardly harsh to Ferdinand and stern towards Miranda, is secretly pleased with how his plan is working. He thanks Ariel for what he has done so far, 'Thou hast done well, fine Ariel', and again assures him of his liberty. But Prospero insists on his absolute authority; Ariel's freedom will be granted only if he performs precisely Prospero's future instructions:

> Thou shalt be as free
> As mountain winds; but then exactly do
> All points of my command. *(lines 497–9)*

Act 1: Critical review

Act 1 is full of contrasts. The violence of the shipwreck in Scene 1 is followed by the calm of the storytelling in Scene 2. But that scene also comprises emotionally charged episodes. Prospero can barely contain his anger as he tells of his overthrow; Ariel delights in how he caused panic on the king's ship, but seems resentful of his continued service, longing for his freedom; Caliban is embittered and angry at his enslavement; but the meeting of Ferdinand and Miranda creates a mood of wonder and mutual love.

Throughout Act 1, the question of rightful authority, a major theme that runs throughout the play, is evident in a variety of examples:

- The Boatswain asserts his command over the king and his court.
- Prospero tells how he was usurped (wrongfully overthrown) as Duke of Milan by his own brother, Antonio.
- Prospero exercises control over Ariel, who longs for freedom, but will only be released when he has fulfilled Prospero's orders.
- Caliban protests that the island is his by right, but that Prospero has stolen it from him.
- Ferdinand, accused of wishing to steal the island, is threatened with dire punishment by Prospero.

Another evident theme is that of imprisonment or confinement: Ariel was painfully confined within a cloven pine, and is threatened with similar imprisonment by Prospero; Caliban is kept like a pig in a sty, confined in a rock; Ferdinand is physically confined by Prospero.

The act also raises important questions about Prospero. Just what does he intend towards his enemies now he has them in his power: will he exact harsh revenge? What kind of a magician is he: does he use his powers for good or ill? As the play unfolds, these questions will recur right up to the final act.

Prospero's rebukes to his daughter Miranda also raise a puzzling question about his relationship with her. In performance, some actors have interpreted his reprimands as those of a strict and emotionally inhibited parent. Others have performed more lovingly tender interpretations.

Act 2 Scene 1

Shakespeare now switches the scene to focus on King Alonso and his court. They have been transported safely by Ariel to a remote part of the island. Alonso is in deep grief, mourning his son Ferdinand, whom he believes is drowned. His courtiers form two distinct groups. Gonzalo (much praised by Prospero in the preceding scene), Adrian and Francisco seek to comfort the king, trying to find good in what has happened to them. In sharp contrast, Sebastian, the king's brother, and Antonio, Prospero's treacherous brother, are cynical and mocking. They joke at Gonzalo's efforts to cheer the king.

Gonzalo tries to encourage Alonso to weigh his sorrow against the relief he can find in their miraculous survival, but the king will not listen, 'Prithee, peace.' Sebastian, in an aside to Antonio, jeeringly puns on the king's words (porridge was made of peas):

> He receives comfort like cold porridge.   *(line 10)*

Sebastian and Antonio continue their ridiculing of Gonzalo's attempts to comfort the king, commenting sarcastically that the good old courtier is 'winding up the watch of his wit', punning on 'entertainer' (person or innkeeper) and on 'dollar' and 'dolour' (sadness). They criticise Gonzalo's talkativeness ('Fie, what a spendthrift is he of his tongue') and contemptuously bet on whether Adrian or Gonzalo will speak first after the king has begged for quiet. Adrian speaks, and the two scoffing courtiers cynically comment on all his optimistic remarks. A brief example shows the sarcastic, negative quality of their style, and the contrast of their characters with the well-intentioned courtiers. They see corruption where others see good:

ADRIAN The air breathes upon us here most sweetly.
SEBASTIAN As if it had lungs, and rotten ones.
ANTONIO Or as 'twere perfumed by a fen.   *(lines 45–7)*

Gonzalo expresses amazement that everyone's clothes are clean and dry in spite of the drenching they received in the shipwreck. His comments reveal that the tempest struck as the court party was returning home to Naples from the wedding of Alonso's daughter Claribel to the king of Tunis. Sebastian comments derisively on the 'sweet marriage' and on how they 'prosper well' in their journey home from it.

The exchanges about 'widow Dido' often prove puzzling to a modern audience. Some knowledge of this famous figure in Roman mythology may help to explain why Jacobeans might have found them humorous. She was Queen of Carthage, and in one version of the myth was faithful to her husband. But in another version, recounted in Virgil's *Aeneid*, she had a passionate affair with Aeneas, the Trojan prince who was believed to have founded Rome. When she was later abandoned by Aeneas, she killed herself. Antonio's and Sebastian's mockery may therefore lie in their amazement at hearing her described as 'widow Dido'. To them it seems an incongruous description, a sign of Gonzalo's lack of sophistication in not knowing Virgil's *Aeneid*. Perhaps Shakespeare wrote the exchange with the more educated members of his audience in mind, who could appreciate the subtlety of the wordplay. Today some actors try to extract humour from the episode by making 'widow Dido' rhyme as 'widow Diddo'.

There is another obscure joke in Gonzalo's mistaking of Tunis for Carthage (which today, and in Shakespeare's time, lies in ruins close to Tunis). In Antonio's and Sebastian's mockery of his references to 'the miraculous harp' and 'raised the wall' (lines 82–3), they are comparing Gonzalo to the legendary Amphian, King of Thebes, who raised the city walls by playing on his harp. Since Gonzalo mistakes Tunis for Carthage, Sebastian is implying that Gonzalo has built the whole city out of words. Once again the joke seems meaningless to a modern audience, and if the lines are kept in the actors rely on their tone of scornful contempt to imply that Gonzalo is once again being disdainfully mocked. The tone, rather than the content, creates the dramatic atmosphere. But Gonzalo persists in his attempt to cheer Alonso, who finally explodes at the comfort he is being offered:

> You cram these words into mine ears, against
> The stomach of my sense   *(lines 101–2)*

Alonso regrets that his daughter was married in Tunis, and feels that the marriage has cost him both his son and his daughter, neither of whom he will see again. His words produce very different responses from Francisco and Sebastian. Francisco claims that Ferdinand probably survived the shipwreck. He had seen the king's son triumphing over the huge waves and successfully swimming towards the shore. Francisco concludes, 'I not doubt / He came alive to land.' After such reassuring optimism, Sebastian's comments are in utter contrast, seeming to wish to wound Alonso's feelings as much as possible. He blames Alonso for all the disasters, and with barely concealed racism claims that all the courtiers begged Alonso not to permit the marriage of Claribel to the king of Tunis, but Alonso preferred to 'lose her to an African'. He hints that Claribel herself ('the fair soul') secretly hated her African husband-to-be, and only married him out of duty to her father's will ('Weighed between loathness and obedience'). Once again Sebastian's unfeeling nature is revealed in his blunt condemnation of his royal brother: 'The fault's / Your own.'

Gonzalo's appeal for Sebastian to speak more compassionately only results in further mockery as the good old courtier seeks to cheer the king with an account of an ideal world where everything is owned in common. Gonzalo's picture of this 'commonwealth' is heavily influenced by an essay entitled 'Of the Cannibals', written by the French philosopher and essayist Michel de Montaigne (1533–92). You can discover on page 68 just how closely Shakespeare followed Montaigne's essay in Gonzalo's description of what he would do if he were king of the commonwealth, in which he says there would be 'No sovereignty', a phrase which evokes the derisory comments of Sebastian and Antonio:

SEBASTIAN   Yet he would be king on't.
ANTONIO The latter end of his commonwealth forgets the beginning.
                                                            (lines 151–2)

But Gonzalo persists with his account of his utopian society in which men and women would live together in natural harmony, kindly provided for by nature, and without the need for governments or armies:

> All things in common nature should produce
> Without sweat or endeavour. Treason, felony,
> Sword, pike, knife, gun, or need of any engine
> Would I not have; but nature should bring forth
> Of it own kind, all foison, all abundance
> To feed my innocent people.   *(lines 153–8)*

After yet more mocking taunts from Sebastian and Antonio, and

Alonso's rebuke that he talks of 'nothing', Gonzalo says that is indeed just what he does. He has told his story simply to give occasion for the two courtiers to 'laugh at nothing'. Gonzalo's stated intention may be true, but his description of the 'commonwealth' reflects Jacobean thinking about newly discovered worlds. It is also central to *The Tempest* itself, in its concerns with ownership of the island and the contrasts of 'civilised' with 'natural' behaviour (see pages 68 and 73).

Ariel's entry introduces the next episode in this 'court' scene, which will show that Antonio and Sebastian are much more malignant than even their derisive sarcasm has suggested so far. The '*solemn music*' that Ariel plays puts Gonzalo, Adrian and Francisco to sleep. Alonso wonders at how quickly they have fallen asleep, but he also feels drowsy and, assured by Antonio's promise that he and Sebastian will keep guard, he too falls into a deep slumber. The action now takes a sinister turn, initiated by Antonio's temptation of Sebastian as the pair regard the sleepers:

> What might,
> Worthy Sebastian, O, what might? – No more.   *(lines 196–7)*

Although Antonio goes on to make clear his murderous intentions, the task for the actor in these few opening words is to convey that from this very moment he intends the death of Alonso. In what follows, the actor playing Sebastian must decide whether to play him as rather stupid, not realising what Antonio is proposing, or whether to play him as verbally fencing with Antonio, knowing that he has assassination in mind, but carefully refusing to declare his own true thoughts until Antonio has fully explained his plan.

Antonio prepares the ground for the planned murder with great subtlety. He asserts that Sebastian is letting his fortune sleep. The imagery the two men use is powerfully suggestive. Sebastian says he is like 'standing water', when the tide is about to turn and neither withdraws (ebbs) nor goes forward (flows). Antonio's 'I'll teach you how to flow' clearly means that he will instruct Sebastian what to do, and when Sebastian responds 'Do so – to ebb / Hereditary sloth instructs me' (I'm naturally lazy), Antonio seizes on this joking comparison, saying it is much more significant than Sebastian suspects, because it implies that idle or fearful people will not succeed in life.

Antonio carries on the 'temptation'. He reminds Sebastian that Ferdinand is drowned, and his death opens up the opportunity for Sebastian's highest hopes to be fulfilled. Alonso's next heir, Claribel, is so far distant that destiny itself invites Antonio and Sebastian to act. Only a messenger moving as fast as the sun could reach her; the journey would take as long as the time from a baby boy being born until he is ready to shave. Claribel dwells

> Ten leagues beyond man's life; she that from Naples
> Can have no note, unless the sun were post –
> The man i'th'moon's too slow – till new-born chins
> Be rough and razorable   *(lines 239–42)*

Antonio proceeds to make his intentions towards the sleepers even more plain:

>   Say this were death
> That now hath seized them, . . .
> . . .
>   O, that you bore
> The mind that I do! What a sleep were this
> For your advancement! Do you understand me?
>   *(lines 253–4, 259–61)*

Sebastian does understand, recalling that Antonio had overthrown his brother Prospero. Antonio points out the power he has gained from the usurpation, 'My brother's servants / Were then my fellows, now they are my men.' He contemptuously rejects all thoughts of conscience, feeling no guilt in having seized Prospero's crown. Twenty consciences could freeze and melt before they might afflict him. He makes his murderous plan utterly plain: he will kill Alonso so that Sebastian can become king. Sebastian must kill Gonzalo to silence any criticism. Antonio displays great contempt for Francisco and Adrian, dismissing them as people who will eagerly follow any instruction, doing whatever is ordered:

> They'll take suggestion as a cat laps milk;
> They'll tell the clock to any business that
> We say befits the hour.   *(lines 281–3)*

Sebastian agrees to the murders and the two villains plan to draw their swords together. The theme of rightful authority suddenly seems about to be played out in a moment of bloody violence. But Sebastian is struck by a sudden thought and moves aside for a private word with Antonio. As they talk, Ariel appears, invisible to those on stage. He has been sent by Prospero to forestall the murders, and he sings in Gonzalo's ear, warning of 'Open-eyed conspiracy'. As Ariel's song ends with 'Awake, awake', Antonio and Sebastian draw their swords, but do not strike because Gonzalo awakes and shakes the king out of his slumber.

Alonso questions the two guilty-looking courtiers, and they, caught with their swords in their hands, make feeble excuses: they heard bellowing, like that of bulls or lions. Audiences often laugh as Sebastian changes his story from 'bulls' to 'lions', because the insincerity and implausibility of the tale is made obvious in performance. Alonso may sound suspicious as he says that he heard nothing, and Gonzalo's report of hearing a strange humming usually adds to the two villains' evident discomfort. Gonzalo and the king are now on guard. They draw their swords and decide to make a further search for Ferdinand. The scene closes with Ariel's couplet in which the final line sounds almost like a benediction on Alonso:

> Prospero my lord shall know what I have done.
> So, king, go safely on to seek thy son. *(lines 319–20)*

Act 2 Scene 2

Caliban is returning to Prospero's cave carrying a burden of wood he has collected. As the noise of thunder is heard, Caliban expresses his resentment against the man who has enslaved him:

> All the infections that the sun sucks up
> From bogs, fens, flats, on Prosper fall, and make him
> By inch-meal a disease. *(lines 1–3)*

He is fearful that Prospero's spirits can hear him, but still cannot help cursing his master. He describes the ways in which Prospero torments him for every minor offence ('every trifle'), causing his spirits to pinch and frighten him, throwing him in swamps and leading him out of his way. They take the form of apes or hedgehogs or snakes, and in these different guises cruelly mistreat him, driving him to madness.

Caliban glimpses Trinculo approaching. Trinculo is King Alonso's court jester, and he has survived the shipwreck, but Caliban mistakes him for one of Prospero's spirits sent to torment him for not bringing in the wood more speedily. Caliban falls flat and covers himself with his cloak. The episode that follows can be wonderfully funny in performance.

Trinculo is fearful of the approaching storm. He can find no natural shelter and suspects that the huge black cloud looming overhead is about to drench him. In what can be a supremely comic moment, he spies the outline of Caliban, lying spreadeagled under the cloak. Some actors, by using delay, double-take or other techniques, have managed to make the audience explode with laughter with only four words: 'What have we here . . . ?' Trinculo speculates, is it a man or a fish? Is it dead or alive? Again, actors can create a gale of audience laughter as they announce their conclusion, arrived at by gingerly lifting the cloak and catching a whiff of Caliban's body odour (poor-John was salted fish):

> A fish, he smells like a fish; a very ancient and fishlike smell; a
> kind of, not-of-the-newest poor-John.   *(lines 24–6)*

Trinculo's next thoughts are of how he could make money out of exhibiting Caliban at English fairgrounds. This reflects a troubling aspect of Jacobean England. The Elizabethan and Jacobean exploration and exploitation of the Americas is strongly echoed in *The Tempest* (see pages 72–5). Explorers sometimes brought inhabitants of the newly-discovered countries back to England. These 'Indians' were often cruelly displayed for profit in fairgrounds and other public places. A painted board would entice every 'holiday fool' to gawp at the so-called 'savages', many of whom died as a result of England's unfamiliar food and cold climate. The exhibitors made large profits from this inhuman practice. Trinculo's 'There would this monster make a man' shows the jester thinking that he could make a fortune from putting Caliban on public show. He comments cynically on how the English more readily spend their money ('doit' = small coin) on demeaning entertainment than on helping the poor:

When they will not give a doit to relieve a lame beggar, they
will lay out ten to see a dead Indian.   *(lines 30–1)*

Trinculo carefully examines Caliban: he has legs and arms like a
man, and is warm. Trinculo decides he has found an islander, recently
killed or stunned by a thunderbolt. Hearing the thunder roll once
again, the fearful Trinculo decides to creep under Caliban's
'gaberdine' (cloak) to take shelter from the storm. As he does so, he
speaks one of the funniest yet most insightful lines in all of
Shakespeare, and the test of any actor is to ensure that the audience
both laughs and recognises the truth of the line:

Misery acquaints a man with strange bedfellows.   *(lines 36–7)*

With Trinculo and Caliban under the cloak, their legs sticking out
from either end, Shakespeare sets the scene for the next comic episode;
and on cue, Stephano arrives, drunk, carrying a bottle and singing.
Stephano is Alonso's butler (wine steward), and he has also survived
the shipwreck but has been drinking the wine he brought ashore. The
drink comforts him, and he is trying to cheer himself further by
singing, even though he recognises the scurviness of the sexual song
he sings so shortly (as he thinks) after so many men's deaths.

Caliban, thinking Stephano is yet an ɪther of Caliban's spirits sent
to torment him, cries out in fear. Stephano drunkenly examines the
curious four-legged object he sees before him. Once again, his
amazed words afford an insight into the attitudes of many Jacobeans
to the original inhabitants of the Americas: 'Do you put tricks upon's
with savages and men of Ind?' (Notice the striking contrast with
Gonzalo's view of native culture expressed in the previous scene, see
pages 19, 68 and 74.)

Caliban still fears torment by Prospero's spirits, and his cry
prompts Stephano to further investigation. He thinks he has found
'some monster of the isle' and, like Trinculo only moments before,
Stephano's thoughts turn to how he can make a profit out of Caliban.
He can ply him with drink, tame him and take him back to Naples,
where he can sell him. Although Shakespeare puts these thoughts
into the minds of two comic characters, he may be criticising what
actually took place when the English colonised America, often treating
the native inhabitants with brutal indifference (see pages 72–5, 96–9).

Prompted by thoughts of gain, Stephano begins to encourage Caliban to drink, 'Open your mouth; here is that which will give language to you, cat' (reflecting the contemporary proverb 'liquor can make a cat speak'). As he pours the wine down Caliban's throat, Trinculo cries out, thinking he recognises Stephano's voice, but fearing that it must be a devil as he thinks the butler is drowned. Stephano is amazed to hear voices coming from each end of the 'monster' and decides to pour more drink down Caliban's throat. But hearing Trinculo's voice, he in turn thinks he has met a devil, and determines to leave because he has 'no long spoon'. Jacobean audiences would recognise the proverb (still occasionally used today) that 'he who sups with the devil needs a long spoon'.

Prompted by Trinculo's further calling, Stephano pulls the jester out from under Caliban's cloak, and expresses amazement that the monster ('moon-calf') can excrete ('siege', 'vent') Trinculos. But Trinculo is simply delighted to find his companion alive, and his joyous response, full of urgent questions and exclamations, is accompanied by vigorous embracings of Stephano, evoking the butler's queasy protest:

> Prithee do not turn me about, my stomach is not constant.
> *(lines 102–3)*

Stephano describes how he escaped the shipwreck, riding on a barrel of wine which he then hid on the seashore, fashioning a bottle from tree-bark to carry a supply of wine with him. Listening to the two Neapolitans, Caliban decides that Stephano must be a god. He pleads for more of the 'celestial liquor' and decides to kneel to Stephano, vowing to be his subject. He asks if Stephano has dropped from heaven, and the butler pompously replies:

> Out o'th'moon I do assure thee. I was the man i'th'moon, when
> time was.   *(lines 124–5)*

Caliban's adoring reply prompts Stephano to offer him more drink, demanding that he swear on the bottle. Trinculo is contemptuous of Caliban: 'a very shallow monster . . . A very weak monster . . . A most poor, credulous monster . . . a most perfidious and drunken monster' (lines 130–7). But Caliban's submission to

Stephano is absolute, and he vows obedience and service to his new-found god:

> I'll show thee every fertile inch o'th'island. And I will kiss thy
> foot – I prithee be my god. *(lines 134–5)*

> I'll kiss thy foot; I'll swear myself thy subject. *(line 138)*

> I'll show thee the best springs; I'll pluck thee berries;
> I'll fish for thee, and get thee wood enough.
> A plague upon the tyrant that I serve!
> I'll bear him no more sticks, but follow thee,
> Thou wondrous man. *(lines 146–50)*

It is valuable to note how this episode echoes and parallels earlier events in the play and certain Jacobean customs or legends which may be unknown to modern audiences:

- *Earlier events* Caliban's promise to serve Stephano loyally seems to echo what happened to Caliban when Prospero first came to the island. Then, too, Caliban was a willing servant and showed Prospero all the fertile places of the island.
- *History* Stephano's story contains an echo of what happened in a real shipwreck, which may have inspired Shakespeare to write *The Tempest* (see pages 65–6). In that shipwreck the sailors heaved barrels overboard.
- *Religion* Stephano's instruction to Trinculo and Caliban to 'Kiss the book' (his bottle) is a parody which echoes the custom of kissing the Bible when promising to tell the truth, or vowing allegiance to a lord.
- *Colonisation* Stephano's claim that he was once upon a time 'the man i'th'moon' echoes what happened as the Americas were colonised. Some settlers, to impress the native people, pretended they came from the moon.

Throughout Caliban's servile submission to Stephano, and Stephano's evident enjoyment of having his foot kissed by a newly-acquired slave who thinks him a god, Trinculo, in a series of asides, keeps up a stream of condemnation of such foolishness. He constantly labels Caliban a 'monster', adding all kinds of pejorative adjectives to the vile description, 'puppy-headed', 'scurvy', 'poor', 'abominable'. He accurately judges the absurdity of what is happening:

> A most ridiculous monster, to make a wonder of a poor
> drunkard.   (lines 151–2)

But Caliban continues with his promise to serve Stephano and share with him the secret resources of the island:

> I prithee let me bring thee where crabs grow;
> And I with my long nails will dig thee pig-nuts,
> Show thee a jay's nest, and instruct thee how
> To snare the nimble marmoset. I'll bring thee
> To clust'ring filberts, and sometimes I'll get thee
> Young scamels from the rock.   (lines 153–8)

No one is really sure what 'scamels' are (they may be shellfish or sea birds), but there is great poignancy in Caliban's eagerness to serve and his willing submission to the drunken Stephano. The poignancy is increased as Stephano decides he will become king of the island ('we will inherit here'), and Caliban, now befuddled with all the wine he has drunk, does not realise he is simply exchanging one master for another. As he bids farewell to Prospero and rejoices in what he thinks is his freedom, his exit song is sadly ironic, ending as it does with a celebratory refrain that is a mere illusion:

> Freedom, high-day, high-day freedom, freedom high-day,
> freedom.   (lines 171–2)

Stephano's 'O brave monster, lead the way!' is simply a command by an ambitious drunkard who thinks he is going to rule the island. Yet again, Shakespeare expresses the theme of rightful authority, this time in a comic yet sinister way. Many productions choose to place the interval at this point, very often with Trinculo and Stephano joining in the refrain of 'freedom high-day'. In one production, Stephano placed a rope around Caliban's neck and led him like a dog on a lead. The stage picture added savagely ironic emphasis to Caliban's re-enslavement.

Act 2: Critical review

Act 2 demonstrates Shakespeare's skill in dramatic construction as he balances the menacing tones of Scene 1 against the comedy of Scene 2. The result is a complex theatrical experience in which the comedy reflects and expresses common themes. The issue of rightful authority, so prominent in Act 1, recurs in both scenes. Antonio and Sebastian concoct their assassination plot to seize power, and Caliban rejects the control of one master only to embrace that of the drunken Stephano. He remains an abject slave. The mood of the play may change but the meaning is cleverly intertwined with what has gone before.

In Gonzalo's 'commonwealth' speech Shakespeare provides a radically different view of rightful authority. In that utopian vision it simply disappears: no government is necessary or desired. Gonzalo's speech also provides a vivid contrast to how Caliban is portrayed. In the ideal commonwealth there are no savages, only peaceful people who live naturally in harmony. As Scene 1 unfolds, that theme of nature versus nurture (or 'civilisation') is given a bitingly ironic twist as the 'civilised' Antonio and Sebastian prepare to murder their way to power.

The episode in which Antonio leads Sebastian into planned bloodshed has been compared with other examples of Shakespeare's 'temptation' scenes: Lady Macbeth spurring on Macbeth to murder Duncan (*Macbeth*); King John prompting Hubert to murder Arthur (*King John*). But Shakespeare is not only drawing upon his own playwriting experience; he also incorporates aspects of the world he knew. Caliban's encounter with Stephano and Trinculo reflects what happened when Europeans colonised the Americas. The Europeans assumed that they were superior to the native people, tried to make money out of them, drugged them with alcohol, and made them their slaves or servants.

Prospero has been absent from the act, but his presence is strongly felt. In Scene 1, through Ariel, he provokes and prevents the murder attempt. In Scene 2, his role as tyrannical slave-owner has been declared and rejected by Caliban.

Act 3 Scene 1

Ferdinand has been set to work by Prospero. His task is to carry logs, the same labour which Caliban has also long performed for Prospero. The scene opens with Ferdinand reflecting on the drudgery he has to perform. He finds pleasure in his toil, and in lines 1–7, in a catalogue of antitheses (contrasting words or expressions, see pages 82–4) sets off the negative aspects of the task with their benefits: 'sports' v. 'painful'; 'labour' v. 'Delight'; 'baseness' v. 'nobly undergone'; 'poor matters' v. 'rich ends'; 'quickens' (brings to life) v. 'dead'; 'labours' v. 'pleasures'.

Ferdinand makes clear that his satisfaction in such hard labour comes from thoughts of Miranda. He expresses her quality in another striking antithesis ('gentle' v. 'crabbed') as he contrasts her with Prospero:

> O, she is
> Ten times more gentle than her father's crabbed –
> And he's composed of harshness.   *(lines 7–9)*

Miranda's tears and comforting words have sustained Ferdinand as he piles up the thousands of logs Prospero has ordered him to shift. Now Miranda appears again, watched by Prospero who is unseen by the young couple. She pleads with Ferdinand not to work so hard, and take some rest. In a romantically extravagant image she wishes the lightning would destroy the logs, which would weep for Ferdinand as they burned. Unaware that her father is watching and listening, she assures Ferdinand that Prospero is asleep, and will not appear for three hours. She offers to carry the logs for him, but Ferdinand prevents her:

> No, precious creature,
> I'd rather crack my sinews, break my back,
> Than you should such dishonour undergo,
> While I sit lazy by.   *(lines 26–9)*

Miranda's protesting reply, saying she would carry the logs with 'more ease' and 'good will' than Ferdinand, evokes a telling aside from Prospero, 'Poor worm, thou art infected'. He recognises the depth and sincerity of her love, shown by her visiting Ferdinand against his

(Prospero's) orders. She is lost to love: he likens her falling in love to catching the plague ('infected').

Ferdinand speaks yet another antithesis, revealing the effect Miranda has on his spirits (''tis fresh morning with me / When you are by at night'). He asks her name, and Miranda once more disobeys her father's order by revealing it. Ferdinand puns on her name, 'Admired Miranda, / Indeed the top of admiration'. In Latin, Miranda means 'to be wondered at', and Ferdinand plays with this meaning in 'Admired' and 'admiration'. In a richly romantic speech he reveals that he has been captivated by many women, but found some fault in every one. Only Miranda is perfect, and beyond compare, without equal ('So perfect and so peerless'). As with all Ferdinand says, the lines present the actor with the task of sounding completely sincere, showing he is genuinely in love. Any trace of irony or modern scepticism would almost certainly destroy the sense of wonder, romance and ideal love that is, it seems, Shakespeare's purpose to create in Ferdinand and Miranda's exchanges.

Miranda's innocence and naivety is evident in her response. She declares she has never seen another woman's face, and the only men she knows are her father and Ferdinand. But she can imagine only Ferdinand as her companion. Her words prompt Ferdinand to declare he is a prince, even a king, and that the log-carrying task is loathsome to him, as unendurable as having 'The flesh-fly blow my mouth'. He says that he fell in love with Miranda at first sight, thinks of himself as her slave, and therefore endures the menial task he has to perform. Her question evokes a declaration from him expressive of the fairytale-like atmosphere of romantic love that Shakespeare has established:

MIRANDA   Do you love me?
FERDINAND O heaven, O earth, bear witness to this sound,
        And crown what I profess with kind event
        If I speak true; if hollowly, invert
        What best is boded me to mischief. I,
        Beyond all limit of what else i'th'world,
        Do love, prize, honour you.   *(lines 69–75)*

Miranda weeps with joy at his words, and the unseen Prospero blesses their love, 'Heavens rain grace / On that which breeds between 'em.' Miranda explains her tears in a somewhat enigmatic way, but then decides to speak directly and plainly ('this is trifling', 'Hence, bashful cunning'). Some critics have noted that Miranda uses an image of pregnancy to describe her way of speaking initially in riddles, 'the more it seeks to hide itself / The bigger bulk it shows'. Although this may seem an unlikely image for the innocent Miranda to use, it looks forward to the masque in Act 4 with its images of fertility and harvest (see page 43). But her open declaration of love is unambiguous and touching:

> I am your wife, if you will marry me;
> If not, I'll die your maid. To be your fellow
> You may deny me, but I'll be your servant
> Whether you will or no. *(lines 85–8)*

The two young people agree to marry, offering their hands and hearts in mutual exchange. They leave vowing to meet in half an hour, and Prospero is left alone on stage where he expresses his pleasure at what has taken place: Miranda and Ferdinand have been astonished and taken unaware by what has happened to them, and Prospero rejoices in their love and forthcoming marriage. But he will return to his books of magic, for he has many relevant matters to prepare ('Much business appertaining'). This probably refers to the arrangements for the wedding masque in Act 4, but also possibly to his arrangements for discomfiting his enemies in Scene 3 of this act.

Act 3 Scene 2

After Scene 1's portrayal of sincere love, the atmosphere once again dramatically changes with the entry of Caliban, Trinculo and Stephano. All three men have been drinking heavily. Stephano demands that Caliban, his 'Servant monster', should drink to him yet again. Trinculo, a little more more sober than his fellow Neapolitan, comments sceptically on his companions' intelligence:

> Servant monster? The folly of this island! They say there's but
> five upon this isle; we are three of them – if th'other two be
> brained like us, the state totters. *(lines 4–6)*

The remark not only causes audience laughter, it hints at the other-worldliness of the island, provoking 'folly' in those who visit it. Even 'the state totters' is another reminder by Shakespeare, albeit in humorous form, of the theme of rightful authority that pervades the play. As Stephano continues to ply Caliban with drink and insist on his own dominance, the theme is comically restated, and underlined by Trinculo's mocking commentary. Stephano boasts of his power ('the sea cannot drown me') and promises to make Caliban his 'lieutenant' or 'standard' (standard bearer). Trinculo puns on 'standard' as meaning 'able to stand', and implies that Stephano will 'list' (keel over like a sinking ship). He continues his ridicule, much to the annoyance of both Caliban and Stephano. Trinculo especially mocks Caliban's calling Stephano 'lord', which proves the 'monster' is a 'natural' (idiot). Stephano's patience breaks and, like the petty tyrant he has become, he threatens to hang the jester:

> Trinculo, keep a good tongue in your head. If you prove a
> mutineer, the next tree. *(lines 32–3)*

Ariel arrives, again invisible to those on stage, and begins to create further trouble for Trinculo. As Caliban (forced to kneel by Stephano) tells his story of his oppression by Prospero, Ariel keeps interjecting, 'Thou liest.' Caliban and Stephano think that it is Trinculo who speaks, and become angrier with each repetition of the statement. Caliban asserts that Prospero stole the island from him by sorcery, and asks Stephano to revenge that injustice and become lord of the isle with Caliban as his servant. He promises to bring Stephano to the sleeping Prospero, 'Where thou mayst knock a nail into his head'.

As Ariel imitates Trinculo's voice, Trinculo protests that he is not the one who makes the accusation of lying, but after repeated threats (e.g. 'I will supplant some of your teeth', 'I'll turn my mercy out o'doors') Stephano finally strikes the bemused jester, and Caliban threatens to do the same. In a plot that reflects Antonio's and Sebastian's plot to kill Alonso, Caliban describes how Stephano can murder the sleeping Prospero:

> Why, as I told thee, 'tis a custom with him
> I'th'afternoon to sleep. There thou mayst brain him,
> Having first seized his books; or with a log
> Batter his skull, or paunch him with a stake,
> Or cut his wezand with thy knife. *(lines 81–5)*

Caliban's catalogue of ways to murder Prospero is a good example of Shakespeare's use of lists (see page 85). Here the list is used to dramatic effect to intensify the evil side of Caliban's character, to show by his enthusiasm for murder the desperate state of mind that a tyrant creates in his subjects, and also to introduce a sinister tension into the play's development (the audience wonders which method they will try).

Caliban insists that Stephano must first seize Prospero's books because they give Prospero his magical powers and enable him to command the spirits that attend on him (but who secretly loathe him). Caliban also tempts Stephano with the prospect of possessing Miranda, a beauty and a 'nonpareil' (without equal). He makes the sexual allurements of the plot quite clear, together with the prospect of establishing a dynasty:

> she will become thy bed, I warrant,
> And bring thee forth brave brood. *(lines 99–100)*

Stephano agrees:

> Monster, I will kill this man. His daughter and I will be king and queen – save our graces! – and Trinculo and thyself shall be viceroys. *(lines 101–3)*

Stephano asks Trinculo how he likes the plan, to which the jester makes the one word reply 'Excellent.' In the 1993 Royal Shakespeare Company production, Trinculo made the audience laugh uproariously by the way he slowly and sarcastically stretched out his reply, 'Ex-cell-ent', clearly showing he thought the idea to be total nonsense. But any irony is lost on Stephano; he asks to shake Trinculo's hand and expresses sorrow that he struck him (but accompanies the apology with a scarcely veiled threat of the consequences that will follow if Trinculo does not 'keep a good tongue in [his] head' in future).

Ariel proposes to reveal the murderous scheme to Prospero, but Caliban, delighted with its acceptance, asks Stephano to sing the song he has recently taught him ('troll the catch' – a 'catch' is a round, in which each person starts singing at a different point). The drunken butler and the jester sing raucously, but Caliban protests, 'That's not the tune', and Ariel adds to the confusion by playing the tune on his tabor (drum) and pipe. Stephano and Trinculo appear terror-stricken by Ariel's music, and Caliban is puzzled by his new master's fear. His reassurance is expressed in one of the most famous and haunting speeches in all Shakespeare, made all the more strangely appealing in that it is spoken by the man described so often by the drunkards as a 'monster', by Prospero as 'filth', and in the list of characters as 'a savage and deformed slave':

> Be not afeared, the isle is full of noises,
> Sounds, and sweet airs, that give delight and hurt not.
> Sometimes a thousand twangling instruments
> Will hum about mine ears; and sometime voices,
> That if I then had waked after long sleep,
> Will make me sleep again; and then in dreaming,
> The clouds methought would open, and show riches
> Ready to drop upon me, that when I waked
> I cried to dream again. *(lines 130–8)*

It is an intensely poignant moment in performance, but this tenderly nostalgic interlude does not last. Stephano breaks the spell with the thought that 'This will prove a brave kingdom to me, where I shall have my music for nothing', and Caliban reverts to brutality with the reminder 'When Prospero is destroyed.' The conspirators leave, following Ariel's music, intent on bloody business.

Act 3 Scene 3

Shakespeare shifts the scene back to the court party. Gonzalo and Alonso are wearied by their travels around the island in fruitless attempts to find Ferdinand. Gonzalo says that his old bones ache and he can go no further. His next words have sometimes been interpreted as symbolising the spiritual journey of King Alonso:

> Here's a maze trod indeed
> Through forth-rights and meanders. *(lines 2–3)*

The interpretation claims that Alonso is wandering in a labyrinth ('maze') unable to find his way out. He is making a symbolic journey on which he will learn, through suffering, to repent his wrongdoings. But at this moment he expresses his tiredness and despair, giving up all hope of finding Ferdinand. He feels mocked by the sea, and acknowledges that his son is drowned. His loss of hope gives comfort to Antonio who draws Sebastian aside, and the two evil conspirators once again agree to murder Alonso that very night when the weariness of the king and his faithful followers will relax their vigilance.

But Prospero has other plans in mind for his enemies, and to 'Solemn and strange music' he enters 'on the top, invisible'. Clearly this stage direction presents a challenge for every production of the play: just what 'Solemn and strange' music should be played, and how should Prospero's entrance 'on the top' be staged? But as Alonso and Gonzalo wonder at the sweet harmony they hear, Shakespeare's next detailed stage direction presents even more imaginative challenges to every director of the play:

> Enter several strange shapes, bringing in a banquet, and dance about it with gentle actions of salutations, and inviting the King, etc. to eat, they depart
> (following line 19)

The 'strange shapes', who are Prospero's spirits in disguise, have been presented in a multiplicity of forms over the centuries. So too, the banquet, the dance, the 'gentle actions of salutations' (saluting Alonso and others), the invitations to eat, and the spirits' departure have also been presented and performed in the widest variety of ways. The stage direction can be thought of as somehow typical of The Tempest itself, in that it constitutes an invitation to every reader, actor, director and designer to imagine for themselves how the play might be performed, and it allows an almost infinite number of legitimate responses to that invitation. The courtiers express their wonder at what they see, and Sebastian's comment catches the mythological quality of the vision:

> A living drollery! Now I will believe
> That there are unicorns; that in Arabia
> There is one tree, the phoenix' throne, one phoenix
> At this hour reigning there.
> (lines 21–4)

A drollery is a kind of puppet show, and the phoenix was a fabulous bird, only one of which lived at any time. It was believed to burn itself upon a funeral pyre ('throne'), and arise, new-born, from the ashes.

Antonio agrees with Sebastian's beliefs, saying that what they have seen was like travellers' tales: the incredible stories that explorers brought back from distant lands; fantasies which were often ridiculed by their hearers. Gonzalo also expresses amazement, saying no one in Naples would believe the story of what he has seen. He praises the gentle manners of the monstrously shaped spirits, kinder than those of many human beings. His comments draw praise from Prospero, who clearly has the evil actions of Antonio and Sebastian in mind ('some of you there present / Are worse than devils').

Sebastian is eager to eat, but first invites Alonso to taste the banquet. Alonso declines, and his refusal prompts Gonzalo to assure him he need not fear. He reminds the king of old beliefs which travellers' tales have now claimed to be true: people living in mountainous regions with goitres (large swellings) below their chins ('Dewlapped like bulls'), and even men whose heads were in their chests (the 'anthropophagi' mentioned in *Othello*, Act 1 Scene 3, lines 143–4). Gonzalo claims that 'Each putter-out of five for one' tells the truth of such beliefs. His phrase refers to the custom in Shakespeare's time of explorers financing their expeditions by betting on the likelihood of their success. They deposited a sum of money before they left on their expeditions, and if they returned safely they could claim five times their deposit.

Alonso is reassured and prepares to eat, inviting Sebastian and Antonio to join him. But as the three men move towards the banquet, Shakespeare's next stage direction provides another startling moment of theatre:

> *Thunder and lightning. Enter* ARIEL, *like a harpy, claps his wings upon the table, and with a quaint device the banquet vanishes*
> (following *line 52*)

It is an awe-inspiring moment. Quite apart from the '*quaint device*' by which the banquet vanishes (perhaps a table with a revolving top in Shakespeare's own theatre), Ariel's appearance as a harpy can be an astonishing presentation. A harpy was a fabulous monster in Greek mythology. It had the head and torso of a woman, and the tail, wings and talons of a bird. In many productions, Ariel has stood, huge wings outstretched, towering over the three terrified aristocrats. His opening condemnation is supernaturally powerful:

> You are three men of sin, whom Destiny –
> That hath to instrument this lower world,
> And what is in't – the never-surfeited sea
> Hath caused to belch up you.   *(lines 53–6)*

Ariel declares the three men unfit to live, and that he has made them mad. As they draw their swords, he reminds them they are powerless, unable alike to wound the wind or the water or a single tiny feather in his plumage ('One dowl that's in my plume'). He and his fellow spirits are invulnerable, for the swords of the three men are now too heavy to lift. He reminds them of their overthrow of Prospero and how they cast him and Miranda adrift on the dangerous sea, for which offence the gods ('powers') have incensed the seas and all creatures against them, causing Alonso to lose his son. As a result, all three now face slow ruin ('Ling'ring perdition'), and only sorrowful repentance and virtuous living can now save them ('heart's sorrow, / And a clear life ensuing'). Another remarkable stage direction follows the end of Ariel's speech of condemnation:

> *Ariel vanishes in thunder; then, to soft music, enter the shapes again,*
> *and dance, with mocks and mows* [pulling faces], *and (then depart)*
> *carrying out the table*   (following *line 82*)

The three men stand transfixed as Prospero congratulates Ariel on his performance. He has followed every instruction to the last detail, as have Prospero's spirits ('meaner ministers'), who have also precisely performed their allotted tasks. Prospero's elation is evident as he sees his plan working out so perfectly, bringing the men who have wronged him under his full control:

> My high charms work,
> And these, mine enemies, are all knit up
> In their distractions. They now are in my power   *(lines 88–90)*

Prospero leaves to visit Ferdinand, and the 'distractions' (madness) of the three wrongdoers is vividly displayed. Gonzalo asks why the king stands 'In this strange stare', and Alonso, jolted into speech, reveals how Ariel's condemnation has deeply struck home. He is in a state of high emotional disturbance, feeling he stands accused by all of nature: 'billows' (waves), 'winds' and 'thunder'. He now experiences an intense sense of guilt at his overthrow of Prospero and thinks his punishment is the loss of Ferdinand. He intends to drown himself alongside his son:

> O, it is monstrous: monstrous!
> Methought the billows spoke and told me of it,
> The winds did sing it to me, and the thunder,
> That deep and dreadful organ-pipe, pronounced
> The name of Prosper. It did bass my trespass;
> Therefore my son i'th'ooze is bedded; and
> I'll seek him deeper than e'er plummet sounded,
> And with him there lie mudded.   *(lines 95–102)*

In contrast, Sebastian and Antonio express no feelings of guilt, but in their own distraction they think they have devils to fight, and each rushes off, determined to resist. Gonzalo, however, judges that all three men are overcome with guilt which works like poison on them. He sends the younger courtiers after them, urging them to prevent any rash action their 'ecstasy' (madness) may provoke them to.

Act 3: Critical review

An atmosphere of wonder pervades the whole act, conveying a powerful sense of the enchantment of the island. In Scene 1, Ferdinand and Miranda declare their love in the language of high romance. In Scene 2, Caliban speaks of his blissful dreams. In Scene 3, Alonso, Antonio and Sebastian are first beguiled by the magical banquet, then driven into distraction by the appearance of Ariel as a harpy delivering his speech of condemnation.

Caliban's dream is an arresting moment in the act. Just as Gonzalo had earlier described a social utopia, Caliban reveals how aspects of the island are like an earthly paradise to him. The action momentarily pauses; the comic drunkards and their antics are temporarily quite out of the audience's focus. Even the business of the bloody plot that has just been hatched seems to disappear from view as Caliban, a lonely, oppressed and dispossessed slave, yearningly expresses the magical and dream-like state of happiness that the island evokes in him. The sympathies of the audience can undergo a radical shift towards empathy with Caliban, the would-be murderer, as he movingly describes with wonder and awe the island's harmony and promise of delight, dreams of peace and riches that are unfulfilled.

But Caliban tells of his dreams in the course of planning a bloody murder. The three drunken characters proceed to provide a comic parody of the theme of usurpation seen earlier in the account of Prospero's ejection from Milan and in the murder plot against Alonso. Stephano tries to behave like a king, and demands his subjects obey him. He threatens to hang Trinculo for mutiny, and finally strikes him. Even Stephano's threat to 'supplant' some of Trinculo's teeth echoes the theme of usurpation, because 'supplant' means 'uproot'.

The characters who appear in Act 3 are all in a state of altered consciousness, but due to very different causes. For Ferdinand and Miranda, love works its transforming power. Stephano, Trinculo and Caliban are affected by drink. Alonso ends the act filled with torturing guilt and remorse, but Antonio and Sebastian seem only 'distracted' by the amazing visions they have witnessed.

Act 4 Scene 1

The scene is set close to Prospero's cell. Prospero has ended the trials to which he has subjected Ferdinand, and now explains why he appeared so harsh. The severe punishment was to test the worthiness and sincerity of Ferdinand's love for Miranda, and Ferdinand has successfully endured the ordeal. Now he has that proof, Prospero gives his daughter ('a third of mine own life') in marriage. His words have raised a puzzling question for some critics: if Miranda is 'a third', what are the other two-thirds of his life? Various suggestions have been made, such as Milan and his books, or his marriage. It has even been speculated that the words give a clue to Prospero's age: Miranda is 15, and he is three times older, 45. Prospero is unambiguous in his praise of Miranda as he gives her to Ferdinand:

> Here, afore heaven,
> I ratify this my rich gift. O Ferdinand,
> Do not smile at me, that I boast her of,
> For thou shalt find she will outstrip all praise
> And make it halt behind her.   *(lines 7–11)*

Prospero's rebuke to Ferdinand (about smiling) has been spoken both kindly and sternly in different productions, but there seems an unmistakable severity in how he delivers his warning about sex before marriage (an injunction that will be repeated later in the scene). He cautions that if the couple have sexual intercourse before marriage, hatred, contempt and strife will follow:

> If thou dost break her virgin-knot before
> All sanctimonious ceremonies may
> With full and holy rite be ministered,
> No sweet aspersion shall the heavens let fall
> To make this contract grow; but barren hate,
> Sour-eyed disdain and discord shall bestrew
> The union of your bed with weeds so loathly
> That you shall hate it both.   *(lines 15–22)*

In Shakespeare's time, the belief that pre-marital intercourse was undesirable was much stronger than it is today. Or rather, it is probably more accurate to say that the public condemnation of the practice was much more vociferous and widespread, because there is evidence that many women (Shakespeare's wife included) were indeed pregnant on their wedding day. Prospero's condemnation is followed by his caution that the young lovers should be guided by the light of the Greek god of marriage ('As Hymen's lamps shall light you').

Ferdinand promises to keep his passions under control, saying he will never do anything, however strong the temptation, to dishonour his marriage with Miranda. Nothing must spoil his wedding day, which will seem slow-moving as if the sun itself stands still ('Phoebus' steeds are foundered' means 'the sun-god's horses have stopped'), making the wedding night itself seem 'chained' (unable to arrive). This was a typical sentiment of marriage songs of Elizabethan and Jacobean times.

Prospero seems content with Ferdinand's assurance, tells him to talk with Miranda, and then summons Ariel. He congratulates Ariel and his fellow spirits ('meaner fellows') on how well they performed at the banquet and harpy illusion, then instructs him to gather together the spirits whom he controls ('the rabble') and prepare another dramatic spectacle, this time for the benefit of Ferdinand and Miranda. Ariel promises to do Prospero's bidding immediately: each spirit will instantly arrive, delicately ('tripping on his toe'), making gestures and pulling faces ('with mop and mow'). Ariel's following line, and Prospero's reply, have been endlessly reinterpreted on stage and in criticism for what they suggest of the relationship between servant and master:

ARIEL Do you love me master? No?
PROSPERO Dearly, my delicate Ariel.   *(lines 48–9)*

Ariel's line has been spoken in the widest variety of ways: sadly, fearfully, playfully, genuinely wishing to know the answer, filled with poignant longing for a loving response, and so on. There are similarly a variety of interpretative possibilities in Prospero's response. It has been delivered offhandedly, sincerely, mockingly. Again, the exchange is one of the many enigmatic moments in the play that are rich in interpretative potential.

Ariel departs to prepare his attendant spirits, and Prospero seems suddenly to snap at Ferdinand, 'Look thou be true! Do not give dalliance / Too much the rein.' He warns his future son-in-law once more about sexual passion. In some modern productions that passion has been all too evident, with Ferdinand and Miranda not simply talking together but locked in an embrace. Ferdinand's reply often provokes a modern audience to hilarity because of its extreme imagery (and because in some performances it is obviously at odds with how the audience has just seen him behaving):

> I warrant you, sir,
> The white cold virgin snow upon my heart
> Abates the ardour of my liver.　　　　　*(lines 54–6)*

It is likely that in Shakespeare's time the lines would have been delivered utterly sincerely and the audience, recognising the Romance tradition within which the play is working at this moment (see page 69), would have accepted the words as entirely befitting the stereotypical chivalrous and pure young lover common to that tradition. Today, every actor playing Ferdinand must decide whether to speak the lines tinged with modern cynicism, or try to convince the audience that he means precisely what he says: that love will overcome his lust.

The actor playing Prospero has a similar decision to make as to how he will speak his single word in response, 'Well.' Again, the word offers the possibility of signifying sceptical disbelief or suspicion (common in modern productions, and often evoking audience laughter) or whole-hearted sincere acceptance that Ferdinand has spoken truly. With an instruction to Ariel to bring as many ('a corollary') spirits as are needed, Prospero orders the masque to begin, and for Ferdinand and Miranda (and the audience) to be fully attentive:

> No tongue! All eyes! Be silent!　　　　　*(line 59)*

For Jacobeans, the masque was a familiar art form. Masques contained spectacular theatrical effects creating striking illusions, music, dance, poetry, and bizarre and mythological characters (for further details see pages 77–8). Your understanding of the nature and function of the masque which Prospero has arranged for Ferdinand and Miranda can be helped if you remember that it symbolises two major themes of *The Tempest*:

- *Harmony after the storm* The appearance of Iris, goddess of the rainbow, expresses the peace that follows a tempest. The rainbow symbolism is abundantly evident. Iris declares herself as the 'watery arch' of 'the queen o'th'sky', and is described by Ceres as 'many-coloured', 'blue bow' and 'Rich scarf to my proud earth'. Just as a rainbow appears after a storm, so Iris herself is an emblem of Prospero's plan: the wedding of Ferdinand and Miranda which will harmoniously unite Naples and Milan after many years of trouble between them.
- *Bounty and fertility* Ceres, goddess of harvest, symbolises the richness that will result from the marriage of Ferdinand and Miranda. For example, the masque begins with Iris describing the fertile natural world over which Ceres ('most bounteous lady') reigns: rich meadows full of crops, mountains with sheep feeding, hay ('stover') fields, flowery river banks ('pionèd and twillèd'), shady woods, pruned ('pole-clipped') vineyards, the seashore ('sea-marge'). Such a lush picture of nature's bounty was a common theme of masques, and here it stands for the fertility which the young couple's union will bring about.

Iris says that Juno ('the queen o'th'sky') commands Ceres to leave her fertile dominions and to join in celebration ('sport') at this very place. Ceres replies by first praising Iris for the rain and beauty her rainbow brings to flowers and woods ('bosky acres'), and then by asking the reason for Juno's command. Iris' explanation is clear:

> A contract of true love to celebrate,
> And some donation freely to estate
> On the blest lovers.   *(lines 84–6)*

Like most Jacobean masques, Prospero's masque draws heavily upon classical mythology, and the sixteen lines that now follow (86–101) present more problems for modern audiences. But your understanding can again be helped if you remember that they echo Prospero's anxiety about Ferdinand and Miranda having sex before marriage. Ceres fears that Venus or Cupid may also join the celebrations, and they had previously plotted that 'dusky Dis' (Pluto, god of the Underworld) would seize Ceres' daughter. For that reason Ceres has sworn she will not tolerate the 'scandalled company' of

Venus or her 'blind boy' (Cupid). Iris reassures her that Venus and Cupid will not be present. She has seen them flying towards Paphos (in Cyprus, a centre of Venus worship), and their plan to make Ferdinand and Miranda misbehave sexually before marriage has been foiled. No 'bed-right' (sexual intercourse) will take place until after the wedding when 'Hymen's torch be lighted'. As a result, Cupid has broken his arrows and vowed to do no more mischief.

Juno now arrives, sometimes in a stunningly theatrical entry, for example descending from the heavens (the roof above the stage) as if by magic. Juno is a moon goddess and protector of women. She invites Ceres to join her, and the two goddesses sing their blessing on Ferdinand and Miranda. Some critics have claimed that it is easy to visualise the goddesses singing their songs of blessing both to the onstage Ferdinand and Miranda, and to the watching Princess Elizabeth and her husband-to-be at a court performance specially for the royal wedding celebrations in 1612–13 (see page 78). They point to the courteous style of the blessings, expressed in formal language, so overflowing with good wishes for joy and a rich harvest in a long marriage (even though other critics point out that the style is typical of many Jacobean masques).

Ferdinand is entranced by the spectacle ('a most majestic vision'), and asks whether the masque is performed by spirits. Prospero assures him that they are indeed spirits who his magic have called up to enact his fantasies ('My present fancies'). Ferdinand is full of happy wonder, expressing unqualified admiration for Prospero, Miranda and the island:

> Let me live here ever;
> So rare a wondered father, and a wife,
> Makes this place paradise.   *(lines 122–4)*

The masque continues with Juno and Ceres whispering together, then sending Iris *'on employment'*. Iris makes clear that her task is to call up water spirits ('naiads') to join in the celebrations of the 'contract of true love' between Ferdinand and Miranda. The nymphs enter at her call and Iris then commands harvesters ('sicklemen') to appear and dance with the nymphs. They too appear, and the *'graceful dance'* that follows again symbolises the theme of fertility and fruitfulness that runs through the masque.

On stage this episode is often a joyous, sunlit occasion, full of light, movement and colour as the water nymphs dance with the straw-hatted, be-smocked harvestmen (they are described as *'properly habited'*, appropriately dressed, in the stage direction). But in the 1993 Royal Shakespeare Company production the dance was given an ominous twist: the faces of the three harvestmen were hidden by their wide-brimmed hats, and as the dance ended they suddenly looked up, revealing to the audience that they were Caliban, Stephano and Trinculo. The theatrical shock gave added impetus to Prospero's sudden recollection of the conspiracy that Caliban has plotted to assassinate him. He recognises that the moment for the killing has almost arrived, and he abruptly orders the end of the masque. Shakespeare's stage direction has the spirits sadly (*'heavily'*) vanishing *'To a strange, hollow and confused noise'*.

Ferdinand and Miranda are puzzled by Prospero's fierce anger, and Prospero's reassurance, urging Ferdinand not to feel troubled, produces one of the most famous speeches in the whole Shakespeare canon. Everything in the masque is ephemeral, and will fade:

> Be cheerful, sir,
> Our revels now are ended; these our actors,
> As I foretold you, were all spirits, and
> Are melted into air, into thin air;
> And like the baseless fabric of this vision,
> The cloud-capped towers, the gorgeous palaces,
> The solemn temples, the great globe itself,
> Yea, all which it inherit, shall dissolve,
> And like this insubstantial pageant faded
> Leave not a rack behind. We are such stuff
> As dreams are made on; and our little life
> Is rounded with a sleep.   *(lines 147–58)*

The speech is full of words with strong theatrical associations: 'revels', 'actors', 'baseless fabric' (like the temporary scenery for a pageant play), 'globe', 'rack' (clouds painted on scenery). Just as the actors have vanished into thin air, so too will everyone and everything else. The lines have become famous as a metaphor for the impermanence of human life. All our achievements, even the world itself, will eventually come to nothing. The mood is elegaic (an elegy is a mournful or reflective poem or song), and every actor playing Prospero attempts to make his delivery as memorable and as moving as possible. But the speech is not simply a theatrical 'set piece'. It is an integral part of the play, reflecting its dream-like quality and its preoccupation with transformation.

The extract is also part of a longer speech, because Prospero goes on to say he is 'vexed', his 'old brain is troubled'. Asking Ferdinand and Miranda to go into his cave, he declares he will walk 'A turn or two' to calm his agitation ('my beating mind'). The young couple leave and Prospero calls up Ariel to question him about Caliban and his accomplices. Ariel (who took the part of Ceres in the masque) describes how he has misled the three drunken conspirators, so intent on murder. Beating his drum, he charmed the would-be assassins into following his music, leading them like cattle through 'Toothed briars, sharp furzes, pricking gorse, and thorns' which painfully scratched their legs, and finally lured them into a stinking pool:

> At last I left them
> I'th'filthy mantled pool beyond your cell,
> There dancing up to th'chins, that the foul lake
> O'er-stunk their feet. *(lines 181–4)*

Prospero congratulates Ariel on his trickery and plans to punish the three men further. He instructs Ariel to fetch 'trumpery' (gaudy clothes) as 'stale' (decoy, con-trick) to hoax them. Prospero then reflects that Caliban is unteachable, his words expressing yet another major theme of the play: can nurture (education, civilisation) change nature? Prospero regrets that in spite of all his training and art he has been unable to improve Caliban:

> A devil, a born devil, on whose nature
> Nurture can never stick; on whom my pains
> Humanely taken, all, all lost, quite lost;
> And, as with age his body uglier grows,
> So his mind cankers. *(lines 188–92)*

Prospero has succeeded in educating Miranda, but has failed with Caliban, so decides to punish him and his confederates further: 'I will plague them all, / Even to roaring.' That process immediately begins as Ariel returns '*laden with glistering apparel*' and is instructed to hang the showy clothing on a line. The scene is set for the next humiliation of the three drunkards, and Prospero and Ariel stand aside to watch the bedraggled men enter. Caliban is still intent on his murderous plan, urging the other two, in a sensitive natural image that is typical of his style, to 'tread softly, that the blind mole may not hear a foot fall'. But the butler and jester are much disillusioned by their experience:

STEPHANO Monster, your fairy, which you say is a harmless fairy,
    has done little better than played the jack with us.
TRINCULO Monster, I do smell all horse-piss, at which my nose is in
   great indignation.   *(lines 196–9)*

They threaten Caliban, who tries to placate them with thoughts of 'the prize' they will shortly achieve. He again urges them to be quiet in another compelling image, 'All's hushed as midnight yet'. But Trinculo and Stephano will not be soothed. They complain bitterly about losing their wine, and again Caliban attempts to mollify Stephano with the thought that, the murder done, the island will be his alone, and Caliban his 'foot-licker' for ever. It seems to work as Stephano declares, 'I do begin to have bloody thoughts.' But Prospero's plan to distract the potential murderers begins to take effect as Trinculo and Stephano become increasingly fascinated by the flashy clothing that Ariel has hung on the line.

Trinculo is first to spot the clothes, and his repeated 'O King Stephano' echoes a song that was popular in Shakespeare's time:

> King Stephen was a worthy peer,
> His breeches cost him but a crown,
> He held them sixpence all too dear
> Therefore he called the tailor lowne (fool).

As the two men eagerly put on the clothing, with Stephano insisting on having the gaudiest gown, all thoughts of murder disappear from their minds, much to the consternation of Caliban who rightly sees the clothing as 'trash'. But the two Europeans are deceived by appearances (another theme of the play). Caliban's urging to do the murder goes unheard as the Neapolitans quarrel and joke over the clothes and the line on which they hang. Their jokes about 'line' (lines

233–8) are usually lost on modern audiences, and actors resort to visual 'business' to try to bring some humour to the episode. In many modern productions the actors speak to the clothes-line itself, moving it about in an attempt to gain laughs through enactment of the text.

Stephano and Trinculo continue with their absurd dressing-up, and Caliban grows increasingly fearful that their fooling will mean the failure of his plan. He imagines Prospero will transform them into something strange and inhuman:

> I will have none on't. We shall lose our time,
> And all be turned to barnacles, or to apes
> With foreheads villainous low.   *(lines 245–7)*

His foreboding proves well-founded because, as the two drunks load him with the garments to carry away, Prospero and Ariel unleash the spirits on them, chasing them around and driving them away. Shakespeare's stage direction provides every production of the play with a wealth of interpretative possibilities in performance, and the moment can be spectacular, sinister and funny all at once:

> *A noise of hunters heard. Enter diverse spirits in shape of dogs and*
> *hounds, hunting them about, Prospero and Ariel setting them on*
> (following *line 252*)

The episode evokes memories of a horrifying feature of the early colonisation of the Americas, when Spanish settlers sometimes used dogs to hunt the natives. Prospero and Ariel spur on the spirits, calling them by hounds' names: Silver, Fury, Tyrant. Prospero, determined to increase the three men's sufferings, instructs Ariel:

> Go, charge my goblins that they grind their joints
> With dry convulsions, shorten up their sinews
> With agèd cramps, and more pinch-spotted make them,
> Than pard, or cat-o'-mountain.   *(lines 255–8)*

The act ends with Prospero reflecting that now all his enemies are within his grasp and at his mercy. He sees his 'labours' shortly at an end, and he promises that then Ariel shall have his freedom. But there remains more service for Ariel to perform.

Act 4: Critical review

Important features of the single scene that comprises Act 4 include:

- Prospero's gift of Miranda to Ferdinand, and his warning against premarital sex;
- the masque celebrating fertility and bounty;
- Prospero's 'Our revels now are ended' speech, symbolising the brevity and impermanence of human life and all other things;
- the foiling of Caliban's murderous plot by beguiling Stephano and Trinculo with trashy clothing;
- the hunting of the conspirators by Prospero's spirits;
- Prospero's claim that his enemies are all at his mercy, and his promise of freedom to Ariel.

These features exemplify major themes or characteristics of the play. Prospero's gift of his daughter underlines the patriarchal control that characterises *The Tempest* (and many other Shakespeare plays). His obsession with sexual abstinence before marriage is echoed in the masque in the exclusion of Venus and Cupid, who plan to tempt Ferdinand and Miranda into sexual misbehaviour. That concern for purity and virginity is a recurring theme of the Romance tradition that influences *The Tempest*.

The masque is also thematically crucial because it reflects Prospero's intentions. Masques ended in the triumph of virtue, with harmony restored under a rightful monarch. That harmony after discord is symbolised in Iris, goddess of the rainbow (the rainbow shows the storm is ended). And the masque's celebration of bounty and fertility represents the children who will be born to Ferdinand and Miranda, creating a dynasty for Prospero and uniting Milan and Naples.

Thoughts of the murderous conspiracy evoke from Prospero a succint statement of another major theme: Caliban is 'a born devil, on whose nature / Nurture can never stick'. The effect of 'nurture' upon 'nature' will be shortly tested when Prospero confronts his enemies. Act 5 will show whether 'nurture' (education, civilisation) is successful in changing the 'nature' of Prospero himself and his 'civilised' enemies: Alonso, Antonio and Sebastian.

Act 5 Scene 1

> Now does my project gather to a head.
> My charms crack not, my spirits obey, and Time
> Goes upright with his carriage.   *(lines 1–3)*

Prospero, outside his cave, foresees the success of all his planning. He is dressed in his magic robes, and his opening lines contain images from alchemy, an early 'science' that attempted to change base metal into gold. An alchemist carried out a 'project' (experiment), which would 'gather to a head' (come to the boil) if it did not 'crack' (fail). The metaphor of alchemy reinforces the idea of Prospero as a magician or magus (see pages 71–2). It is worth pausing to reflect on just what the aims of Prospero's project might be:

- *politics* to regain his dukedom and unite Naples and Milan through the marriage of Miranda and Ferdinand;
- *revenge* to punish Alonso, Antonio and Sebastian;
- *repentance* to bring these 'three men of sin' to repent of their wrongdoings;
- *reform* to overcome, through nurture (education, civilisation), the wicked nature of others;
- *self-knowledge* to deepen his own humanity by overcoming his own nature, learning to prefer mercy to vengeance;
- *reward* to release Ariel from his service;
- *escape* to leave the island to return to Milan;
- *harmony* to achieve unity and peace in personal, social and natural life.

Ariel reports that the time is 'On the sixth hour', suggesting that all the action of the play has so far taken place within four hours (see page 90). But he accompanies the information with the reminder that this is also the time that 'our work should cease'. In some productions Ariel has spoken the line resentfully as a clear reminder that the time for his freedom is now overdue. But Prospero merely confirms that he promised their work would end at six, and asks after Alonso and the courtiers. Ariel reports their troubled state: Alonso, Sebastian and Antonio are 'all three distracted' and the rest of the court mourn sorrowfully over their leaders' apparent madness. Gonzalo is weeping copiously, his tears falling down his beard 'like winter's drops / From eaves of reeds'.

The exchange that follows has been seen by some critics as the moral centre of the play, when Prospero learns from Ariel's compassion for the troubled wrongdoers that mercy and forgiveness are preferable to vengeance and anger:

ARIEL   Your charm so strongly works 'em
  That if you now beheld them, your affections
  Would become tender.
PROSPERO   Dost thou think so, spirit?
ARIEL Mine would, sir, were I human.
PROSPERO   And mine shall.
  Hast thou, which art but air, a touch, a feeling
  Of their afflictions, and shall not myself,
  One of their kind, that relish all as sharply
  Passion as they, be kindlier moved than thou art? *(lines 17–24)*

In the theatre it can be an intensely affecting episode. Prospero often pauses for a long time, clearly reflecting on Ariel's 'Mine would, sir, were I human.' Audiences can be much moved by the sight of Prospero's inward struggle as he comes to terms with what he is hearing: that an unearthly, insubstantial spirit can feel pity for the suffering of men, however evil, when he himself, fully human, has not yet achieved that capacity for compassion. Prospero's declaration 'And mine shall' shows he has at last made that empathic step, as he determines to end his punishment of his enemies. A few lines later he acknowledges that although he has been deeply hurt by the injustice done to him, his 'nobler reason' must triumph over his 'fury'. His decision that mercy is preferable to revenge is memorably expressed:

    The rarer action is
 In virtue, than in vengeance.   *(lines 27–8)*

In *The Tempest*, the word 'virtue' has many associations: mercy, forgiveness, magnanimity, humanity, love, reason, good faith. All these benign associations, but particularly the first, are evident in Prospero's declaration for mercy rather than retribution. He judges that all his enemies are now penitent (a judgement that will shortly be shown to be questionable) and that his aims have been fulfilled. He therefore orders Ariel to release Alonso and the others, and decides to break his spell that enchants them, restoring them to their former selves. Ariel leaves, and Prospero, alone on stage, appeals to the spirits who have helped him to perform miracles and declares he will give up his magical powers.

He begins his invocation to the spirits by listing them, 'Ye elves of hills, brooks, standing lakes, and groves . . .' (lines 33–40). It is a dazzling catalogue of Prospero's helpers, showing the range of magical workers who inhabit the natural world and produce strange features that so puzzled human beings from the earliest times, for example 'fairy rings' in the grass and mushrooms that appear overnight.

Prospero next lists all the miracles that the spirits ('Weak masters') have enabled him to perform. His supernatural powers, learned through his secret studies, are awesome: dimming the sun, creating tempests, lightning and earthquakes, and bringing the dead back to life. Again, the sheer power of the speech is reinforced by the accumulation of items, listing astonishing superhuman achievement upon achievement. Once again Prospero's role as magus (see page 72) is established, even if the play itself has shown only his power to raise the violent sea tempest. Of his claim that he can raise the dead, the play provides no evidence, but it is likely that many in his Jacobean audiences would have found his words profoundly disturbing because such a practice was associated with sorcery and witchcraft. As Shakespeare wrote this speech, he clearly had before him a copy of Ovid's *Metamorphoses* open at the speech by the sorceress Medea. Page 67 shows how closely Shakespeare 'imitated' what he read, but transformed it into his own electrifying dramatic verse.

After his long invocation to the spirits and the description of his awe-inspiring powers, Prospero declares he will give up his supernatural powers. He calls for soothing music that will release Alonso and the others from their distraction, resolves to break his magic staff and drown his mystical books in the deepest ocean. He will once again become a mere mortal:

> But this rough magic
> I here abjure. And when I have required
> Some heavenly music – which even now I do –

> To work mine end upon their senses that
> This airy charm is for, I'll break my staff,
> Bury it certain fathoms in the earth,
> And deeper than did ever plummet sound
> I'll drown my book. *(lines 50–7)*

Many critics have argued that the lines represent Shakespeare's farewell to the theatre. For example, they claim that 'I'll drown my book' could mean 'I'll end my playwriting'. It is an appealing, but fanciful notion and is really only a matter of belief (and Shakespeare went on to co-write *The Two Noble Kinsmen* and *King Henry VIII*). But occasionally a production embraces the theory, and presents Prospero looking remarkably like the popular image of Shakespeare.

Note: on pages 109–15 you will find a further analytic discussion of all that has happened so far in lines 1–57.

After Prospero's call for music and his decision to 'drown my book', most productions have him use his staff to trace out a large circle on the stage. Into this circle the court party enter, and Shakespeare again provides a detailed and enigmatic stage direction inviting imaginative interpretation. It has been performed in a multiplicity of ways:

> *Solemn music. Here enters* ARIEL *before; then* ALONSO *with a frantic gesture, attended by* GONZALO; SEBASTIAN *and* ANTONIO *in like manner attended by* ADRIAN *and* FRANCISCO. *They all enter the circle which Prospero has made, and there stand charmed; which Prospero observing, speaks* (following *line 57*)

Prospero begins by praising the music, which will cure the madness from which Alonso, Sebastian and Antonio suffer, their brains boiled within their skulls. Prospero speaks to each man in turn, none of whom can hear him because they are still charmed ('spell-stopped'). First Prospero praises Gonzalo, 'honourable man', and sheds friendly tears to match the honest old courtier's own weeping. Acknowledging that Gonzalo saved his life and is a loyal servant of Alonso, Prospero promises to reward the faithful counsellor.

Next Prospero addresses Alonso, recalling the cruelty with which the king of Naples had treated both himself and Miranda. He turns to Sebastian, who had been an accomplice to that cruelty and who is now 'pinched' (tormented) for his wicked action. But when Prospero speaks to his brother, Antonio, the commitment to mercy which Ariel has caused him to embrace, becomes evident. Beginning with condemnation of Antonio's evil nature, Prospero (often after a long pause in line 78) finds it possible to forgive his 'Unnatural' brother. Antonio may lack contrition and kindness, but Prospero grants him mercy:

> Flesh and blood,
> You, brother mine, that entertained ambition,
> Expelled remorse and nature, who, with Sebastian –
> Whose inward pinches therefore are most strong –
> Would here have killed your king; I do forgive thee,
> Unnatural though thou art.   *(lines 74–9)*

The music now begins to disperse the charm that holds Alonso and the courtiers as in a trance. Prospero decides that when they fully awake they shall see him as the duke of Milan. He sends Ariel for his hat and rapier, and again promises the spirit he shall have freedom. Ariel quickly returns and helps to dress Prospero in all his finery. As he dresses his master he delights in the prospect of soon having his freedom, and sings of a future of everlasting summer ('After summer' probably means following summer perpetually around the earth):

> Where the bee sucks, there suck I;
> In a cowslip's bell I lie;
> There I couch when owls do cry;
> On the bat's back I do fly,
> After summer merrily.
> Merrily, merrily, shall I live now,
> Under the blossom that hangs on the bough.   *(lines 88–94)*

In performance it can be a moment of tender affection between master and servant, and Prospero can reinforce that impression in his kindly response:

> Why that's my dainty Ariel. I shall miss thee,
> But yet thou shalt have freedom.   *(lines 95–6)*

Ariel is sent to fetch the sailors, who are all asleep in the king's ship. As Ariel leaves on his mission, the courtiers are released from their enchantment, and Gonzalo probably speaks for all of them as he expresses fear at the torments they have experienced. But the fearful mood gives way to wonder and amazement as Prospero presents himself, 'Behold, sir king, / The wrongèd Duke of Milan, Prospero'. It must be a fraught moment for his enemies as they see standing before them the man they had so grievously wronged many years ago. But Prospero immediately displays his friendship by embracing Alonso and welcoming everyone.

Alonso is profoundly affected by the sight of his former enemy. He suspects at first that his madness might still be magically tricking him. Prospero's embrace assures him that it is no enchanted vision but a real man who he sees. Alonso realises his madness has passed, and he instantly resigns all claim to Milan and begs Prospero to pardon all the wrongs he has done against him. He asks to know how Prospero has survived and now appears on the island. Significantly, Prospero does not reply, but turns to embrace the still amazed Gonzalo. Prospero acknowledges Gonzalo's limitless honour, and assures him that his wonder is a natural response to this magical island.

After again welcoming everyone, Prospero privately warns Antonio and Sebastian that he has knowledge of their murderous plot, which, if revealed to Alonso, would put their lives at peril. He then publicly forgives Antonio and demands back his dukedom. The context of Prospero's forgiveness suggests that it is offered with great difficulty, between clenched teeth:

> For you, most wicked sir, whom to call brother
> Would even infect my mouth, I do forgive
> Thy rankest fault – all of them – and require
> My dukedom of thee, which perforce I know
> Thou must restore.   (lines 130–4)

Significantly, Shakespeare gives Antonio no words in reply. Each actor playing Antonio must decide how to respond, so that the audience can form an impression of his feelings towards the brother he deceitfully usurped. Indeed, Antonio's virtual silence throughout this final scene (in which he speaks only two lines) is one of the many curious features of the play that affords actors and readers a multiplicity of imaginative possibilities from which to construct their own preferred interpretation. Many modern productions have portrayed Antonio as sullenly unrepentant for his wrongdoings.

Alonso again asks Prospero to tell them how he has survived to meet them on the island. He remarks that it is only 'three hours since' that he himself was shipwrecked and how heartbroken he is that he has lost his son Ferdinand in the wreck. Prospero expresses sorrow for Alonso's loss and reveals that he has suffered a 'like loss': his own daughter is lost. The grief-stricken Alonso is stunned by the news and wishes that he himself were drowned and Ferdinand and Miranda were alive and married, reigning as king and queen of Naples. He questions Prospero when he lost his daughter and receives the reply 'In this last tempest.' Many critics have noted how the words 'lost', 'loss' and 'lose' recur throughout the exchange between Alonso and Prospero. Some argue that Shakespeare was deliberately using these repetitions to echo certain Christian beliefs familiar to his Jacobean audiences: that loss is necessary in order to find God, and that redemption and forgiveness can come only through the suffering that loss entails.

Prospero comments again on the courtiers' astonishment at seeing him. He once more assures them that he is the usurped duke of Milan who arrived 'most strangely' on the islai d and is now lord of it. But he puts off telling his full story until a later time. For the third time he welcomes Alonso, and invites him to look into his cave where, in return for having returned Prospero's dukedom, Alonso will see something good: 'a wonder, to content ye'. The stage direction reveals the nature of that 'wonder' (a pun on Miranda's name):

Here Prospero discovers FERDINAND *and* MIRANDA, *playing at chess*
(following *line 171*)

In the Jacobean theatre, Prospero probably drew a curtain at the back of the stage to reveal the lovers, but modern productions have staged all kinds of ways in which he 'discovers' them. For example, in the 2002 Royal Shakespeare Company production they were drawn in seated in a boat, the chess set between them. In Shakespeare's time chess was an aristocratic or royal game, and here the significance may be to suggest their future as rulers of Naples. Miranda accuses

Ferdinand of cheating, but the accusation may be in order to prompt a response which suggests unqualified love between the couple:

FERDINAND No, my dearest love, I would not for the world.
MIRANDA Yes, for a score of kingdoms you should wrangle,
      And I would call it fair play.   *(lines 173–5)*

Alonso can scarcely believe his eyes, and even the villainous Sebastian is moved to describe the sight as 'A most high miracle.' Ferdinand's joy at seeing his father whom he had thought dead is evident as he kneels before Alonso and acknowledges the mercy of the seas in sparing him. Miranda is equally moved, but for a different reason. She has lived for twelve years on the island, seeing only Prospero and Caliban. Now, at the sight of the king and his court she expresses her marvel in another of the play's most memorable speeches:

                                    O wonder!
    How many goodly creatures are there here!
    How beauteous mankind is! O brave new world
    That has such people in't!   *(lines 181–4)*

Miranda's wonder at the sight of so many 'goodly' strangers is charged with dramatic irony. The 'beauteous mankind' she sees includes people who have treated her and her father foully. They are usurpers and would-be murderers. Aldous Huxley's novel *Brave New World* uses Miranda's words ironically to describe a far from human future world. Prospero's brief response to Miranda's delighted exclamation can be (and often is) delivered to underscore that irony:

    'Tis new to thee.   *(line 184)*

Alonso questions his son about Miranda, thinking she might be the goddess of the island who has engineered both their separation and reunion. But Ferdinand assures him that Miranda is indeed mortal, is his wife and Prospero's daughter. Alonso is much moved, feeling he must ask pardon from Miranda for the wrong he has done her, but Prospero urges that all past sorrows should be forgotten. It is now the turn of Gonzalo to thank the gods for having brought them all to the island. He invites the gods to 'drop a blessèd crown' on Ferdinand and Miranda. Gonzalo rejoices in the happy outcome, and claims that every person has found himself or herself in the voyage and shipwreck:

> O rejoice
> Beyond a common joy, and set it down
> With gold on lasting pillars: in one voyage
> Did Claribel her husband find at Tunis,
> And Ferdinand her brother found a wife
> Where he himself was lost; Prospero, his dukedom
> In a poor isle, and all of us ourselves,
> When no man was his own.   *(lines 206–13)*

It is a remarkably optimistic interpretation of what has happened. Gonzalo's speech is typical of those in the Romance tradition that celebrate the happy outcomes that follow all adversities. In that tradition characters learn from their ordeals, and increased self-knowledge and understanding result from suffering. But modern interpretations, on stage and in criticism, draw attention to Sebastian and Antonio who give little or no sign that they have been changed for the good by their experience. Nonetheless Alonso keeps up the mood of joyous celebration and blesses Ferdinand and Miranda, but in a way that may suggest he delivers his second and third lines at Sebastian and Antonio:

> Give me your hands:
> Let grief and sorrow still embrace his heart
> That doth not wish you joy.   *(lines 213–15)*

Ariel now leads in the evidently astonished Master and Boatswain. Gonzalo jokingly greets the Boatswain reminding him of what he had said during the shipwreck (that the Boatswain was destined to hang on shore, not to drown, see pages 5–6). After declaring how delighted he is to have found that the king and his court are safe, the Boatswain tells a story full of striking detail. The ship is 'tight and yare' (shipshape and ready to sail); all the crew were asleep, imprisoned below deck ('clapped under hatches'), and they were wakened by the weirdest variety of noises. They found themselves free, the ship undamaged, and saw the Master dancing with delight at the sight. The Master and Boatswain have been suddenly separated from the crew and have, as in a daze ('moping'), now been brought before their king.

Ariel hopes for praise from Prospero for what he has done. He obtains it ('Bravely, my diligence') and is yet again promised his freedom. Alonso is further amazed by what he has seen and heard. It seems inexplicable. But Prospero promises that he will soon, at leisure, make all clear. Ariel is dispatched to fetch Caliban, Stephano and Trinculo, and Prospero reminds Alonso that 'Some few odd lads' of his ship's company are still missing. His words are the cue for Ariel to drive in the three men, Caliban, Stephano and Trinculo, wearing the gaudy clothes they took from the line. Stephano is still drunk, shouting vague commands. Trinculo, also drunk, and Caliban, in very different ways, are impressed by what they see (Setebos is regarded by Caliban as the god of himself and his mother, Sycorax):

TRINCULO If these be true spies which I wear in my head, here's a
goodly sight.
CALIBAN O Setebos, these be brave spirits indeed!
How fine my master is! I am afraid
He will chastise me. *(lines 259–63)*

Sebastian and Antonio return to their old cynical style, so evident in their first appearance in the play. They comment on the men's strange appearance and market value. Antonio's remark that Caliban is 'no doubt marketable' echoes the thought that both Stephano and Trinculo expressed when they first encountered him, and again reflects the Jacobean custom of exhibiting 'monsters' at freak shows (see page 23). Prospero explains just who the three are, and how they plotted against his life. He tells Alonso that:

Two of these fellows you
Must know and own; this thing of darkness, I
Acknowledge mine. *(lines 274–6)*

Many critics believe that Prospero's words about Caliban ('this thing of darkness') imply much more than ownership: that the islander is his servant. They argue that Prospero accepts that he too has an evil side to his nature, and that his exile on the island has taught him that. He may even be acknowledging that he is responsible for turning Caliban into a 'thing of darkness'.

Caliban fears he will be pinched to death, but the drunken Trinculo jokes about his own condition: he is so pickled in alcohol that death will not affect him, the liquor will keep him from 'fly-blowing' (decay). Stephano is already suffering from the cramps, and in response to Prospero's taunt ruefully comments that if he had been king of the island he 'should have been a sore one'. Prospero orders Caliban to take the drunkards to his cave, and to behave well in future if he expects pardon. Caliban's final words seem to express contrition and a desire for wisdom and grace. He recognises his foolishness in mistaking the drunken Stephano as a god:

> Ay that I will; and I'll be wise hereafter,
> And seek for grace. What a thrice-double ass
> Was I to take this drunkard for a god
> And worship this dull fool!   *(lines 293–6)*

The three bedraggled men stagger off, taunted by a final sardonic insult from Sebastian that they have stolen the gaudy clothes. Prospero invites Alonso and the court to spend the night in his cave, where he will make the time pass quickly by telling of all that has happened to him on the island. Tomorrow he will accompany them to their ship and they will all set sail for Naples where they will see the formal marriage of Ferdinand and Miranda. He will then travel back to Milan, where:

> Every third thought shall be my grave.   *(line 310)*

Like so many aspects of the play, Prospero's statement is enigmatic. It may mean he will be preoccupied with death, or that his other thoughts will be for Milan, or for Ferdinand and Miranda and the children they will surely have.

Alonso looks forward to hearing Prospero's life story, and again Prospero agrees to recount every detail. He ends the action of the play by promising a favourable voyage so speedy that they will catch up with the rest of the fleet already bound for Naples. He instructs Ariel to ensure that happens, and then finally grants the spirit's freedom:

> I'll deliver all,
> And promise you calm seas, auspicious gales,
> And sail so expeditious that shall catch
> Your royal fleet far off. My Ariel, chick,
> That is thy charge. Then to the elements
> Be free, and fare thou well. Please you draw near.
>
> *(lines 312–17)*

Just how the characters leave the stage can create powerful impressions in the minds of the audience. Perhaps the most obvious problem is that of portraying the exit of Sebastian and Antonio. Shakespeare has given them no words of remorse or repentance, and each production has to take its own decision about which of a wide range of attitudes they might show. Ariel's departure poses a similarly intriguing puzzle. In many Victorian productions he flew off delightedly in a spectacular aerial display, sometimes singing his 'Where the bee sucks' song. But in a memorable Royal Shakespeare Company production he spat scornfully in Prospero's face to show what he really thought of his demanding master. In striking contrast, a famous Oxford outdoor production had Ariel running joyfully across the surface of a lake into the darkness.

Epilogue

The performance has not yet ended. Prospero's final 'Please you draw near' is usually spoken direct to the audience, inviting them to listen to the Epilogue. Prospero now finds himself in the same position as Ariel and Caliban. He must plead to a superior power (the audience) for his freedom. He admits all his magical powers have gone:

> Now my charms are all o'erthrown,
> And what strength I have's mine own –
> Which is most faint.
>
> *(lines 1–3)*

It was a convention in many Elizabethan and Jacobean plays for an actor to step out of role at the end and ask for applause. But Prospero seems to stay in role, hoping to be released from the island so that he may journey to Naples. Nonetheless he does ask for applause, and again admits his lack of 'Spirits to enforce, art to enchant'. So he ends with a plea, calling on the mercy of the audience, asking them to pardon him as they too would wish to be pardoned (and as he has pardoned his enemies). The word that has echoed through the play recurs as the final one to be spoken, 'free':

> And my ending is despair,
> Unless I be relieved by prayer
> Which pierces so, that it assaults
> Mercy itself, and frees all faults.
> As you from crimes would pardoned be,
> Let your indulgence set me free.   *(lines 15–20)*

What usually follows is audience applause. But a few modern productions have ended with a final tableau that raises directly the question that has haunted the play: who owns the island? In such productions, Caliban returns, menacingly or blankly enigmatic, to face Prospero, and the lights fade on that scene of confrontation. Caliban seems about to re-inherit the isle. In one production, both Ariel and Caliban returned, confronting each other silently, implying that a further struggle for domination is about to begin. Such directorial inventions lie outside the text and their frequency in recent years is yet another demonstration of how every age interprets and stages Shakespeare to reflect its own interests and preoccupations (see the Critical approaches section, pages 88–106).

Act 5: Critical review

In traditional interpretations of Act 5, the major themes of the play are seen as harmoniously concluded. Prospero learns from Ariel the virtue of forgiveness over vengeance and grants mercy to his enemies; reconciliation is achieved; rightful authority is restored; magic is renounced; and liberty is granted as characters are set free from their enchantments or confinements. Prospero and the others prepare to return to Naples, and the ownership of the island reverts to Caliban, who will 'seek for grace'.

But Shakespeare's playwriting skill puts such neat and optimistic conclusions into question. He fills the act with complexities, silences, ironies and ambivalences:

- Neither Sebastian nor Antonio express remorse or show that their characters have been reformed.
- Prospero's public forgiveness of Antonio is begrudgingly spoken, and he threatens he may later expose his brother's and Sebastian's murderous intentions.
- Miranda's few speeches suggest she has much learning to do. She willingly accepts any cheating or deception Ferdinand might practise as 'fair play'. In her 'O brave new world' speech, the men she describes as 'beauteous' include usurpers and potential killers (Prospero ironically replies ''Tis new to thee').
- Prospero's renunciation of his 'rough magic' raises troubling questions about the nature of his supernatural powers. Raising the dead was often thought of as black magic, and his speech disturbingly echoes that of the sorceress Medea (see page 52).
- Ariel makes no response to being finally set free. His attitude towards his master Prospero remains enigmatic.
- Prospero becomes Duke of Milan once more, but through the marriage of Ferdinand and Miranda, Milan is still subject to Naples.
- It remains unclear what will happen to Caliban.

Act 5 is therefore typical of *The Tempest* itself: a hauntingly open text which invites the reader or actor to 'fill in the blanks' that Shakespeare leaves. The many contradictory possibilities in performance enable you to create your own interpretations and 'closures'.

The hugely enjoyable film *Shakespeare in Love* portrays a popular belief about the source of Shakespeare's creativity. It shows him suffering from 'writer's block', unable to put pen to paper, with no idea of how to write his next play. But all is resolved when he meets a beautiful young girl. His love for her sparks an overwhelming flow of creative energy – and he writes *Romeo and Juliet*!

It is an attractive idea, and the film presents it delightfully, but the truth of the matter is far more complex. Like every other writer, Shakespeare was influenced by many factors other than his own personal experience. The society of his time, its practices, beliefs and language in political and economic affairs, culture and religion, were the raw materials on which his imagination worked.

This section identifies the contexts from which *The Tempest* emerged: the wide range of different influences which fostered the creativity of Shakespeare as he wrote the play. These contexts ensured that *The Tempest* is full of all kinds of reminders of everyday life, and the familiar knowledge, assumptions, beliefs and values of Jacobean England.

What did Shakespeare write?

Scholars generally agree that Shakespeare wrote *The Tempest* some time around 1610–11. What was the play that Shakespeare wrote and his audiences heard? No one knows for certain because his original script has not survived, nor have any handwritten amendments he might subsequently have made. So what is the origin of the text of the play you are studying? *The Tempest* was first published in 1623 (seven years after Shakespeare's death) in the volume known as the First Folio which contains 36 of his plays. It is the first play in the Folio and seems carefully edited, two features that have led some critics to speculate that Shakespeare's fellow actors John Heminges and Henry Condell, who prepared the Folio, regarded the play very highly indeed.

Today, all editions of *The Tempest* are based on the First Folio version. But the edition of the play you are using will vary in many minor respects from other editions. That is because although every editor of the play uses the Folio version, each one makes a multitude of different judgements about such matters as spelling, punctuation, stage directions (entrances and exits, asides, etc.), scene locations and other features.

So the text of *The Tempest* is not as stable as you might think. This is no reason for dismay, but rather an opportunity to think about how the differences reflect what actually happens in performance. Every production, on stage or film, cuts, adapts and amends the text to present its own unique version of *The Tempest*. This Guide follows the New Cambridge edition of the play (also used in Cambridge School Shakespeare).

What did Shakespeare read?

Shakespeare's genius lay in his ability to transform what he read into gripping drama. This section is therefore about the influence of genre: the literary contexts of *The Tempest* (what critics today call 'intertextuality': the way texts influence each other). It identifies the stories and dramatic conventions that fired Shakespeare's imagination as he wrote *The Tempest*.

The Tempest is one of only four of Shakespeare's plays for which there is no clearly identifiable dominant source for the plot (the other three are *A Midsummer Night's Dream*, *Love's Labour's Lost* and *The Merry Wives of Windsor*). For example, all scholars agree that *Romeo and Juliet* emerged from Shakespeare's reading of a long poem by Arthur Brooke, *The Tragicall Historye of Romeus and Juliet*, first published in 1562. Shakespeare's genius as a dramatist and poet was to turn Brooke's tedious poem into soaring verse and thrilling theatre. No such major source has been found for *The Tempest*, and Shakespeare seems, unusually, to have conceived the plot himself.

But it is clear that as he wrote *The Tempest* Shakespeare was influenced by many secondary sources such as travel documents, the works of Ovid (a Roman poet, 43BC–AD17), which he had studied at school and whose influence is detectable in every play, the essays of Montaigne, and also by what is known as the Romance tradition.

In writing *The Tempest*, Shakespeare drew upon a true story which became well known through three documents widely read in London in autumn 1610. The story they told began in May 1609 when a fleet of nine ships set out from England. Five hundred colonists were on board. Their goal was the newly founded colony of Virginia, where the settlers intended to begin a new life. They hoped for fabulous fortunes because of everything they had heard about the natural riches of America. But disaster struck the voyage.

In a great storm, the flagship of the convoy, the *Sea Venture*, carrying the expedition's leader, Sir Thomas Gates, became separated from the fleet. The ship was driven onto the rocks of Bermuda, a place feared by sailors and known at the time as the Devil's Islands ('the still-vexed Bermudas' of Act 1 Scene 2, line 229). The rest of the fleet sailed on, reached Virginia and sent back news to London of the loss of the expedition's leader with all of his 150 companions.

For almost a year England mourned the loss. Then, in the late summer of 1610, the astonishing news arrived that the lost colonists had miraculously survived the shipwreck and had reached Virginia. The *Sea Venture* had run aground close to shore, and all the passengers and crew had escaped safely. They discovered that Bermuda was far from being the desolate and barren place of legend. It had fresh water and a plentiful supply of food in fish, wild pigs, birds and turtles. The survivors set about building two boats so that they could sail on to Virginia.

It seemed as if providence smiled. But human nature soured the good fortune of the survivors, and mutiny broke out. There were attempts to seize the stores. Malicious rumours spread, and a bid was made to murder Sir Thomas Gates and take over the island. One mutineer was executed. Only after great difficulties did Gates and his companions set sail for Virginia.

Shakespeare almost certainly found his inspiration for *The Tempest* in the three documents which circulated in London in late 1610. They described the misadventures of the colonists. William Strachey's *A True Reportory of the Wrack and Redemption of Sir Thomas Gates* was available in manuscript (it was not published until 1625). Sylvester Jourdan's *Discovery of the Bermudas*, and the Council of Virginia's *True Declaration of the Estate of the Colony in Virginia* were printed pamphlets. The play directly echoes a number of features in the tale of the shipwreck and the survivors' experience.

Shakespeare's reading of the Roman poet Ovid is also evident in *The Tempest*. Ovid's best-known work is his *Metamorphoses*, a collection of stories telling of miraculous transformations. Shakespeare knew *Metamorphoses* very well indeed and it has been estimated that around 90% of all the allusions to classical mythology in his plays and poems refer to tales in Ovid's epic collection. He often uses Ovid's stories of bodily changes (e.g. a man into a stag) as images or parallels of the psychological changes his characters undergo and the emotional turmoils they endure. Shakespeare most clearly draws upon Ovid in Prospero's renunciation of his rough magic (Act 5 Scene 1, lines 33–57). As the following short extracts show, Prospero's speech is Shakespeare's 'imitation' (or rather transformation) of what Ovid wrote for the sorceress Medea.

> Ye elves of hills, brooks, standing lakes, and groves,
> . . .
> by whose aid –
> Weak masters though ye be – I have bedimmed
> The noontide sun, called forth the mutinous winds,
> And 'twixt the green sea and the azured vault
> Set roaring war. To the dread rattling thunder
> Have I given fire, and rifted Jove's stout oak
> With his own bolt; the strong-based promontory
> Have I made shake, and by the spurs plucked up
> The pine and cedar; graves at my command
> Have waked their sleepers, oped, and let 'em forth
> By my so potent art.
>
> *(Act 5 Scene 1, lines 33, 40–50)*

Ye elves of hills, of brooks, of woods alone,
Of standing lakes, and of the night, approach ye every one,
Through help of whom (the crooked banks much wond'ring at the thing)
I have compelled streams to run clean backward to their spring,
By charms I make the calm seas rough and make the rough seas plain,
And cover all the sky with clouds and chase them thence again.
By charms I raise and lay the winds and burst the viper's jaw,
And from the bowels of the earth both stones and trees do draw.
Whole woods and forests I remove; I make the mountains shake,
And even the earth itself to groan and fearfully to quake.
I call up dead men from their graves; and thee, O lightsome moon,
I darken oft, though beaten brass abate thy peril soon;
Our sorcery dims the morning fair and darks the sun at noon.

(Ovid, in Arthur Golding's translation, 1567)

The Tempest also contains two clear examples of passages where Shakespeare drew upon the writings of the French humanist and essayist Michel de Montaigne (1533–92). The first is when Prospero decides that mercy is preferable to revenge ('The rarer action is in virtue, than in vengeance'), which contains strong echoes of Montaigne's essay 'Of Cruelty'. But an even more striking example is in Gonzalo's account of an ideal world where everything is owned in common. Gonzalo's picture of this 'commonwealth' is heavily influenced by Montaigne's essay entitled 'Of the Cannibals'.

Shakespeare had obviously read the essay, in which Montaigne argued that the 'savage' societies being discovered in the New World (America) were superior to the sophisticated civilisations of Europe. The European adventurers were the real barbarians, even though they were confident of their moral superiority. The essay helped give rise to the belief in 'the noble savage', for whom peaceful, equal and harmonious relationships were completely natural. Unlike the colonists, they lived in accordance with nature.

A comparison of the first part of Gonzalo's description with a contemporary translation of Montaigne shows just how closely Shakespeare followed what he read, but made subtle alterations, additions and omissions to turn it into dramatic verse:

> no kind of traffic
> Would I admit; no name of magistrate;
> Letters should not be known; riches, poverty,
> And use of service, none; contract, succession,
> Bourn, bound of land, tilth, vineyard, none;
> No use of metal, corn, or wine, or oil;
> No occupation, all men idle, all;
> And women too, but innocent and pure;
> No sovereignty –   *(Act 2 Scene 1, lines 143–51)*

> It is a nation . . . that hath no kind of traffic, no knowledge of letters, no intelligence of numbers, no name of magistrate nor of political superiority, no use of service, of riches or poverty, no contracts, no successions, no dividences (partitions of land), no occupation but idle, no respect of kindred but common, no apparel but natural, no manuring of lands, no use of wine, corn or metal.   (Montaigne)

The Tempest can also be seen as part of the development of Shakespeare's playwriting career. Although he transformed English drama, he was always alert to what audiences liked, and responded to popular taste. For example, very early in his playwriting career, bloodthirsty tragedies were the fashion, and he wrote the immensely successful *Titus Andronicus* (some time between 1590 and 1594). Now, close to the end of his professional career, the taste was for tragicomedy, which drew on what is now called the Romance tradition.

The Romance tradition had largely derived from stories of love and chivalry which were very popular in the Middle Ages, for example tales of King Arthur, the *Song of Rolande, Roman de la Rose* and Chaucer's *Knight's Tale.* It dealt with the trials of young knights, and presented two views of love: courtly (sexless, idealised, faithful) and romantic (also idealised and unsexual, but including 'love at first sight'), of which marriage was seen as the natural result. Romance stories had typical ingredients: forests where magical transformations occurred, journeys to exotic places, magical events, adventures, trials and testing through which learning occurred; all kinds of coincidences and fairytale improbabilities; harsh fathers with beautiful daughters; disguise and mistaken identity; and happy endings with forgiveness, reconciliations, and virtue triumphant.

All these features can be detected in some form in *The Tempest*, and at the time that Shakespeare wrote the play, Romance had become a much-enjoyed dramatic genre with its own specific features additional to those just listed. These included sea voyages and storms, lucky and unlucky accidents, children lost and found, years of searching and grief, and the resurrection of loved ones long thought dead.

What was Shakespeare's England like?

Like all writers, Shakespeare reflected in his plays the world he knew. His Jacobean audiences, watching performances of *The Tempest*, would recognise many aspects of their own time and place. This section begins with a few brief examples of particular allusions, then provides more extended discussion of features of Jacobean England that have importance for understanding the play as a whole.

Obvious examples include words which had meanings for Shakespeare's contemporaries but are now rarely, or never, in use. For example, Alonso describes himself as 'heavy', meaning 'sleepy'; the spirits who carry out the banquet make 'mocks and mows', insulting gestures and faces; Caliban wishes that Stephano will cut Prospero's 'wezand', windpipe or throat; Ariel beats his 'tabor', drum; the Boatswain in the final scene describes the ship as 'tight and yare', shipshape and ready to sail.

Other features of the play evoke Shakespeare's Jacobean world. In the opening scene, many of Shakespeare's contemporaries would recognise that the Boatswain's commands very accurately reflect the nautical language in use at the time. In the same scene, when Antonio curses the Boatswain and hopes he 'mightst lie drowning / The washing of ten tides', they would recall the current practice that pirates were condemned to be hanged and afterwards have at least three tides wash over their bodies. And when, in the play's second scene, Prospero tells his story of how his brother Antonio, acting as duke, learned 'who / To trash for over-topping', a modern audience might understand this as meaning that Antonio threw out over-ambitious courtiers. However, Jacobeans knew that 'trash' meant 'to rein in a dog', so their understanding of Prospero's meaning was somewhat different from its interpretation today.

Similarly, Jacobeans would recognise everyday proverbs and contemporary practices in phrases which puzzle modern audiences and readers. In Act 2 Scene 1, Antonio and Sebastian continually mock Gonzalo. He becomes exasperated and exclaims that they 'would lift the moon out of her sphere' (lines 175–6). His exclamation echoes the contemporary proverb that 'the moon still shines in spite of all the barking of dogs'. When Sebastian immediately retorts, 'We would so, and then go a-batfowling', Shakespeare's audience would have no problems in seeing the significance: birds were often caught by attracting them with light and striking them with sticks (bats). Sebastian is saying that he and Antonio would use the stolen moon as such a light to catch fools like Gonzalo. Jacobean legislation is evident in the same scene. When Sebastian mockingly salutes Gonzalo with "Save his majesty!' (line 163) instead of 'God save his majesty!', this is because a Jacobean law forbade oaths which used God's name.

In addition to such topical reminders of everyday life, there are other ways in which *The Tempest* reveals what Jacobean England was like. Important social and cultural contexts that influenced the creation of *The Tempest* include magic and science, colonialism, travellers' tales, politics, the masque.

Magic and science

Throughout Shakespeare's lifetime, witches were the object of morbid and fevered fascination. A veritable witch mania characterised the reign of Elizabeth I, and many witches (mainly women) were tried and sometimes burned to death. Although some voices were raised against such barbarous persecution, most people believed in witches. Hundreds of pamphlets describing details of witchcraft trials were printed and sold. King James was as fascinated by witchcraft as any of his subjects. In 1590 a group of witches tried to kill him. Their plot was discovered and they were brought to trial at Berwick. James personally interrogated one of the witches. Fired by his experience he personally investigated other witchcraft cases. In 1597 he published *Demonology*, a book on witchcraft. When he became King of England in 1603, he ordered its immediate printing in London.

Shakespeare's *Macbeth* (1606) had already drawn upon this public and royal interest in witchcraft, and the play had achieved great success. Now, in *The Tempest*, he returns to the topic, but enlarges his focus to encompass different types of magic. The play is full of magic and its effects. The opening tempest, which seems so real, is only an enchantment. Strange shapes, fantastic creatures and wonderful illusions appear. Music pervades the play, mesmerising characters. Ariel's song expresses the mysterious transformations which take place, as everything undergoes 'a sea-change, into something rich and strange'.

During Shakespeare's lifetime, the frontiers of knowledge greatly expanded as scientific enquiry advanced year by year. In Europe during the fifteenth and sixteenth centuries, the movement known as the Renaissance, the rediscovery of classical learning, sparked off dazzling advances in artistic and scientific discovery and creativity (historians today tend to use the expression the 'early modern period' rather than the 'Renaissance'). But the line between science and magic was not clearly drawn. Magician-scholars were legendary, most famously Doctor Faustus, who sold his soul to the Devil in exchange for magical powers. Scientists often investigated (and sometimes believed in) the supernatural.

When Shakespeare created Prospero he may have had in mind Doctor John Dee, a famous English scholar, mathematician and geographer who had died in 1608. For the first half of his career Doctor Dee was highly respected, but he increasingly fell into suspicion and disgrace, and died reviled and embittered. Some of his work was scientific, but his extensive library also included many books on the occult. He was widely regarded (and feared) as a 'magus', a man of great learning who also dabbled in magic, and who could exercise control over both the natural and supernatural world (Dee claimed he could conjure up archangels, but was widely regarded as practising 'black magic'). A magus was somewhat like an astrologer and sorcerer, who communicated with the occult or spirit world.

Prospero can be seen as a magus. He has devoted his life to secret studies in order to gain magical powers, his 'art'. He has control over earth, air, fire and water. He can raise and calm tempests, command his spirits to produce fantastic banquets and masques, make himself invisible, and control Caliban with cramps and pinches. He can call up music, and send other characters to sleep. When he decides to renounce his magical powers, Prospero recalls all the miracles he can perform: dimming the sun, commanding the winds, creating storms at sea, splitting oaks with lightning bolts, and causing earthquakes. He can even raise the dead from their graves. That last power, necromancy, communicating with the dead, has a sombre implication: it was believed to be the essence of 'black magic', the art of Sycorax. Yet, elsewhere in the play Prospero seems concerned to stress that all his magical powers are benign and so give him moral authority.

Colonialism

The Elizabethan and Jacobean periods, with the voyages of discovery and the colonisation of the 'New World' (the Americas), experienced a huge expansion of knowledge of the geographical world. But that expansion of knowledge was accompanied by oppression and exploitation of the peoples of the newly discovered lands. The history of the colonisation of the Americas was often a story of horror and savagery. Although some Europeans tried to uphold the principle of benign civilisation, the overwhelming evidence is that of brutal conquest.

The Tempest has been interpreted, particularly in modern criticism and performances, as a dramatic exploration of the philosophical, moral and political questions raised by the impact of Europe on the New World. Most crucially, these questions concern themselves with the right of Europeans to subjugate the native inhabitants, enslave them and profit from the seizure of their land and resources. How the European colonisers treated the 'natives' depended upon whether they viewed them as 'savages' or as human beings equal to themselves.

Many Europeans believed it was their divinely ordained task to take ownership of the New World. They felt confident they were educating the uneducated, bringing spiritual enlightenment to the heathen, and extending the domains of their European monarchs. Hand in glove with these aims went the profitable exploitation of what was seen as a wilderness, neglected by its native inhabitants. But it must have looked very different through the eyes of the indigenous peoples. They saw their freedom vanish as their lands were seized and their old religions destroyed. Millions found themselves forced into virtual slavery.

The Europeans sought to prosper through trade, exploiting the rich resources of the New World. Land which the native inhabitants regarded as their own was seized by gun and sword. Resentful of Prospero's take-over, Caliban claims 'This island's mine', to which Prospero replies 'Thou most lying slave'. Trinculo wonders how much money he might get by exhibiting Caliban at an English fair. Similarly, Sebastian and Antonio comment mockingly on Caliban's market value (Act 5 Scene 1, lines 264–6). European greed was a driving force of so-called 'civilisation', but the colonists from Europe found their beliefs and culture challenged by their experience of the Americas, and so greed was compounded by the desire to dominate and assert the superiority of western religion, ethnicity and language.

A major aim of colonisation was to spread the Christian gospel. The native Americans were seen as heathens who worshipped false gods. Caliban is described as a son of the Devil and a witch (Act 5 Scene 1, lines 268–73). He worships the Patagonian god Setebos. Colonisation was seen in part as a religious crusade sanctioned by God. However harsh the settlers' treatment of the natives, it was often justified by the claim that the intention was to save their souls, and bring them to the true religion.

European Christians also believed in their ethnic superiority over the native races of the New World. Such people were seen as savages or cannibals (Caliban is almost an anagram of 'cannibal'). They were regarded as treacherous by nature, repaying kindness with deceit. Even the colour of their skin was held to be a mark of their less-than-human status ('this thing of darkness' as Prospero describes Caliban).

Many colonists thought that such people could legitimately be treated as useful slaves ('He does make our fire, / Fetch in our wood', Act I Scene 2, lines 312–13).

Throughout history, conquerors and governments have tried to suppress or eliminate the language of certain groups, defining it as 'inferior'. Within living memory, Welsh children were forbidden to speak their native language in school. The ancient Greeks called anyone who did not speak Greek a 'barbarian' (speaking 'baa-baa' languages). In Shakespeare's time, many Europeans believed that only their own languages were 'civilised'. The mark of savagery was not knowing English or Spanish or some other European language. Overseas languages were 'gabble', without real meaning. Caliban must be taught Prospero's language in order to know his own meaning. Caliban uses it vividly to express the resentment of the enslaved, 'You taught me language, and my profit on't / Is, I know how to curse.'

The Tempest reflects much of colonial experience, especially in the relationship of European and native as master and servant or slave. Like Caliban, the native inhabitants often revealed the natural resources of their lands to the newcomers, only to have ownership of those resources stripped from them by force. Colonialism is therefore necessarily bound up with questions of authority and rightful rule which echo through the play: who does have the right to rule, whether on the island or in Milan or Naples?

Some critics accuse Shakespeare of giving a Eurocentric view of colonisation in *The Tempest*. They argue that the story is told only from Prospero's point of view. Caliban has only limited opportunities to tell his side of the story of harsh subjugation, of how the master–slave relationship quickly replaced that of teacher–pupil. However, Shakespeare, echoing Montaigne, also gives voice to a quite different view of the New World in the play. Gonzalo's description of the commonwealth (Act 2 Scene I, lines 142–58) is that of an ideal world, a benign utopia of peace and harmony.

Today most critics argue that *The Tempest* is strongly influenced by the colonisation of the Americas. But some have asserted that it strongly parallels African or Irish colonial experience. For example, although the play contains no mention of Ireland, Dympna Callaghan has made a powerful case for how *The Tempest* reflects the English imposition of colonial rule on Ireland. The native Irish were dispossessed and exploited, and regarded as subhuman savages whose language was a barbarous gabble. Such treatment provoked huge resentment and active resistance. Callaghan argues that Ireland in many ways exemplifies the questions that *The Tempest* raises about colonial settlement, legitimate political rule and revenge.

Travellers' tales

Travellers' tales were common in Jacobean England as explorers, sailors and traders brought back stories of their experiences in new-found countries. Pamphlets and oral reports often exaggerated and distorted the nature of the native inhabitants, their customs and culture, and the land itself. The grotesque portrayal of Caliban by Trinculo and Stephano ('strange fish', 'monster', 'mooncalf', etc.) reflects the baleful influence of such travellers' tales. Two kinds of tales seem particularly relevant: those concerned with social class and with sexuality.

- *Social class* The notion of social hierarchy was firmly fixed in the European mind. Most people believed it to be God-given. At the top was the king, who claimed to rule by divine right. Below him were aristocrats, courtiers, and so on down to the lowest peasant. The 'masterless man' (a person without a superior) was seen as a terrible threat to social order. The European colonists of the New World brought back reports that the natives lived without a rigid social hierarchy, each man the equal of others. To Prospero, Caliban represents potential anarchy, and must therefore be controlled by harsh punishment.

- *Sexuality* Travellers' tales reported that the marriage customs of Europe were quite unknown in the Americas. In the colonists' eyes, debauchery and vice flourished without control among the natives. To the Europeans, such free love was abhorrent. In this European view, Caliban's attempted rape of Miranda is evidence of his fundamentally evil nature, justifying constraint and harsh punishment. From the same viewpoint, Prospero's strict control of the sexual relations of Miranda and Ferdinand expresses the moral values of a higher state of civilisation, characterised by restraint, abstinence and self-discipline.

Whereas Montaigne (see page 68) interpreted native free love as demonstrating their essential innocence, most Europeans took it as an indication of their depravity. Caliban cannot see what was wrong with his attempt to have sex with Miranda. Shakespeare makes him do what natives were believed to do, and Prospero, like most Europeans, is appalled by the action.

Politics

Unlike many other of his plays, *The Tempest* does not seem clearly to treat political aspects of Shakespeare's England other than that of colonialism. At a general level some of its themes are the preoccupations of the times, particularly the issue of rightful authority. But it seems difficult to connect the play directly to Jacobean politics. Nonetheless, it has been argued that certain aspects of the play have contemporary parallels.

- *Prospero as King James* In *Basilicon Doron* (a book on government that James I wrote for his son), the king warned his son that a monarch should not be too absorbed in his studies because that would make him neglect his royal duties.
- *Arranged royal marriages* Just as Prospero is concerned to unite Milan and Naples through the marriage of Miranda and Ferdinand, so too King James was much concerned to arrange marriages of state for his own children to forge or strengthen political alliances. In the play, Alonso had, against the wishes of his court, arranged the marriage of his daughter (a Christian) to the king of Tunis (presumably a Muslim). King James, as part of his political statecraft, attempted to marry his devoutly Protestant children Henry and Elizabeth to Catholics. Both attempts failed: Prince Henry died, and as Elizabeth's planned marriage was part of the 'deal' (Henry was to marry a princess of Savoy, Elizabeth a prince of Piedmont), that too was abandoned. She was married in 1612 to the Protestant Frederick the Elector Palatine (and lived out her life as 'the winter queen' of Bohemia). Some politically aware members of Shakespeare's audience would recognise that royal marriages as a tool of diplomacy are reflected in the wedding that will end the 'inveterate' enmity of Milan and Naples.
- *The influence of Machiavelli* A few critics have seen evidence in the play of Shakespeare's knowledge of Italian politics, and the writings of Niccolò Machiavelli (1469–1527), whose book *The Prince* (1532) was a handbook for rulers about the use of deceit in

statecraft. Machiavelli urged rulers to consider any means, however unethical or immoral, to stay in power. This 'Italian politique' approach centres on Prospero's usurpation by his brother Antonio, a machiavellian figure who encourages Sebastian to gain the throne of Naples by murder. Even the discovery of Ferdinand and Miranda playing chess, and Miranda declaring she willingly accepts Ferdinand's cheating, have been interpreted as an acknowledgement of Italian *realpolitik* (power politics). Nigel Smith (see Resources section, page 126) gives a very readable account of this particular political interpretation of the play.

- *Ariel as spy* Some critics have argued that Prospero's use of Ariel as his informer and agent parallels the tight system of state surveillance and spying established under Queen Elizabeth and maintained by King James.

The masque

The Tempest may also be, in part, Shakespeare's response to the masque, a type of theatre which became very popular during the reign of King James I. The masque in Act 4 can be, for many modern spectators and readers, the most difficult part of the play. But for Jacobeans it was a familiar and fashionable art form, probably the favourite entertainment at court (with the queen and courtiers sometimes taking part), and also much enjoyed by theatre audiences. Masques contained spectacular theatrical effects, music, dance and bizarre characters. They revelled in visual effects, with striking set designs, complex stage machinery and lighting (in indoor stagings), all creating remarkable illusions. Masques were rich in elaborate scenery and gorgeous costumes. They were often very expensive affairs. King James I spent £20,000 on one masque alone, over £1 million today.

For Jacobeans, such entertainments possessed an iconographic significance that is lost on modern audiences. King James and his court would have expected a masque to end in the triumph of virtue, peace and beauty, with harmony restored under a rightful monarch (in Prospero's masque the appearance of Iris, goddess of the rainbow, symbolises such peace after storm). Jacobean masques were full of references to, and characters from, classical mythology. The commentary on pages 42–4 shows how Prospero's masque displays such features.

Court masques were often devised to celebrate a particular event, such as a royal birthday or marriage. It has sometimes been claimed that the masque in *The Tempest*, indeed the play itself, was written to be part of the marriage celebrations in the winter of 1612–13 for Princess Elizabeth, daughter of King James I. This is disputed because there is a record of a previous performance at court on 1 November 1611. Another argument against this claim is the fact that Shakespeare's acting company, The King's Men, had been performing in their own indoor theatre, the Blackfriars, from 1608, and the argument goes that this 'indoor' work greatly contributed to the development of masques. Today, most critics do not accept that the play was written especially for the wedding, pointing to the fact that 13 other plays were performed during the ceremonies – including *Othello*.

Shakespeare's own life

Many critics have taken the view that Shakespeare was writing about himself when he created the role of Prospero (see page 89) and that through the play he was bidding farewell to his art as a playwright. In particular, the lines in the Epilogue 'Now my charms are all o'erthrown, / And what strength I have's mine own' are sometimes argued to be Shakespeare's professional leave-taking as he retires to Stratford-upon-Avon (but he collaborated on two further plays in his 'retirement').

This section began with the film *Shakespeare in Love*. It is a delightful fantasy which gives the impression that the inspiration for *Romeo and Juliet* was Shakespeare's own personal experience of falling in love. Today, critics and examiners give little or no credit to approaches which interpret *The Tempest* in the context of Shakespeare's emotional life, because nothing is really known of his intimate thoughts, feelings or activities. Today the focus of critical attention is on social and cultural contexts such as those identified in this section.

Language

Ben Jonson famously remarked that Shakespeare 'wanted art' (lacked technical skill). But Jonson's comment is mistaken, as is the popular image of Shakespeare as a 'natural' writer, utterly spontaneous, inspired only by his imagination. Shakespeare possessed a profound knowledge of the language techniques of both his own and earlier literary ages. Behind the apparent effortlessness of the language lies a deeply practised skill. That skill is evident in *The Tempest* in all kinds of ways. The play displays a wide variety of language registers, sometimes formal or elaborate, sometimes earthy, always flexible and subtle. Each character is given their own distinctive voice, and the songs subtlely echo the play's themes and moods. Jacobeans would recognise all such qualities as 'decorum': appropriate language for event, mood and character.

Shakespeare wrote *The Tempest* at almost the end of his playwriting career, and the play's brevity (only *The Comedy of Errors* is shorter) displays his mastery of the linguistic skills he had acquired. The style is very different from his early plays. The language is sometimes compressed and dense, often enigmatic and ambiguous. There are irregular rhythms and word orders, and different verb tenses are sometimes used in the same sentence. There are many hyphenated compound words ('sea-swallowed', 'hag-born', 'sight-outrunning'). Shakespeare may have used these hyphenated words because their instability expresses the sense of wonder and ever-changing reality that runs through the play. Linking words together with a hyphen expands the meaning of the resulting compound and can, at the same time, increase ambiguity. Occasionally words or syllables are omitted which, together with elisions ('hearts i'th'state', 'in lieu o'th'premises'), increases the sense of urgency or intensity of feeling. In his troubled agitation, Prospero fails to complete a sentence (Act 1 Scene 2, lines 77–87). Such features and the recurrence of many different references to sleep, dreams and enchantment help to create the island's air of mystery and illusion.

What follows are some of the language techniques Shakespeare uses in *The Tempest* to intensify dramatic effect, create mood and character, and so produce memorable theatre. As you read them, always keep in mind that Shakespeare wrote for the stage, and that actors will therefore employ a wide variety of both non-verbal and verbal methods to exploit the dramatic possibilities of the language. They will use the full range of their voices and accompany the words with appropriate expressions, gestures and actions.

Imagery

The Tempest abounds in imagery (sometimes called 'figures' or 'figurative language'): vivid words and phrases that help create the atmosphere of the play as they conjure up emotionally charged pictures or associations in the imagination. When Prospero describes his brother Antonio as 'The ivy which had hid my princely trunk, / And sucked my verdure out on't', Antonio's gradual destruction of Prospero's power is vividly conveyed in the image of how ivy covers and weakens a mighty tree. Shakespeare seems to have thought abundantly in images, and the whole play richly demonstrates his unflagging and varied use of verbal illustration, as when Antonio describes how King Alonso and his courtiers fell asleep: 'They dropped, as by a thunder-stroke'.

Shakespeare's imagery uses metaphor, simile or personification. All are comparisons which in effect substitute one thing (the image) for another (the thing described).

- A *simile* compares one thing to another using 'like' or 'as'. Sebastian mocks Alonso's refusal to be cheered, 'He receives comfort like cold porridge'; Trinculo exclaims that Caliban 'smells like a fish'; and Ariel describes Gonzalo's weeping like rain falling from a thatched roof, 'His tears runs down his beard like winter's drops / From eaves of reeds.' Similarly, Prospero describes Ariel's torment of imprisonment in the cloven pine, 'where thou didst vent thy groans / As fast as mill-wheels strike'; and Antonio contemptuously remarks how readily Alonso's courtiers will follow a new master, 'They'll take suggestion as a cat laps milk'.

- A *metaphor* is also a comparison, suggesting that two dissimilar things are actually the same. Ferdinand describes his punishment of carrying logs as 'This wooden slavery'; for Miranda, her modesty is 'The jewel in my dower'; and Prospero describes Caliban as 'this thing of darkness'. He uses another haunting image for the past, 'the dark backward and abysm of time'.

To put it another way, a metaphor borrows one word or phrase to express another. For example Antonio's murderous dagger becomes 'this obedient steel'; the leaky boat in which Prospero and Miranda were set adrift is 'A rotten carcass of a butt', and his copious weeping on their perilous voyage is memorably pictured in 'When I have decked the sea with drops full salt'. Antonio uses a remarkable image of human growth from babyhood to manhood to express the long passage of time before Claribel learns of Alonso's death, 'till new-born chins / Be rough and razorable'.

- *Personification* turns all kinds of things into persons, giving them human feelings or attributes: 'bountiful Fortune' brings Prospero's enemies within his reach, and 'Time / Goes upright'.

Early critics, such as John Dryden and Doctor Johnson, were critical of Shakespeare's fondness for imagery. They felt that many images obscured meaning and detracted attention from the subjects they represented. Over the past 200 years, however, critics, poets and audiences have increasingly valued Shakespeare's imagery. They recognise how he uses it to give pleasure as it stirs the audience's imagination, deepens the dramatic impact of particular moments or moods, provides insight into character, and intensifies meaning and emotional force. Images make the familiar strange and carry powerful significance far deeper than their surface meanings. Certain images recur and the following paragraphs suggest how the varying imagery of the sea, the theatre and nature pervade the play, deepening its atmosphere of recurring transformation, of illusion and of the fertility of the island.

The sea

The Tempest begins in a storm and ends with the promise of calm seas. In between, images of the sea recur frequently: 'sea-sorrow', 'sea-change', 'sea-swallowed', 'never-surfeited sea' (suggesting the infinite appetite of the ocean), 'still-closing waters', 'sea-marge' and so on. Immediately after the shipwreck, Miranda's first words describe 'the wild waters' and tell of the sea dashing out the lightning (Act 1 Scene 2, lines 1–5). Prospero speaks of the tempest which he and Miranda endured when they were banished from Milan, 'th'sea, that roared to us'. The sea's ebb and flow is reflected in the exchange in which Antonio tempts Sebastian ('I am standing water', 'I'll teach you how to flow', 'Ebbing men, indeed', Act 2 Scene 1, lines 213–20). And Prospero, about to release his enemies from their enchantment, declares:

> Their understanding
> Begins to swell, and the approaching tide
> Will shortly fill the reasonable shore
>
> *(Act 5 Scene 1, lines 79-81)*

The theatre

Shakespeare's interest in the theatre is evident throughout *The Tempest*. There are spectacular dramatic events such as the shipwreck, the banquet and the masque. The language is full of echoes of acting and plays. Ariel is like a stage-manager as he 'performs' the tempest and arranges the banquet and the masque. When he seizes control in Milan, Antonio is like an actor who would 'have no screen between this part he played, / And him he played it for' (Act 1 Scene 2, lines 107–8). Later, as he plots Alonso's murder, Antonio uses the language of the theatre: 'cast . . . perform . . . act . . . prologue . . . discharge' (Act 2 Scene 1, lines 243–6). Prospero reflects on the way in which life itself is like a stage pageant, whose actors and theatre, 'the great globe itself', vanish into thin air (Act 4 Scene 1, lines 147–58).

Nature

The play abounds in language that evokes the rich variety of the natural world: sea, air, earth and wildlife, thunder and lightning, wind and roaring water. Every scene contains many aspects of nature, both benign and threatening, and Caliban's language expresses his intimate knowledge and love and fear of the island's natural life: 'fresh springs, brine-pits, barren place and fertile', 'pig-nuts', 'jay's nest', 'clust'ring filberts', 'Young scamels', 'adders', 'hedgehogs', 'wicked dew', 'raven's feather' and many others. Ariel delights that he has led the drunken conspirators through 'Toothed briars, sharp furzes, pricking gorse, and thorns' to the 'filthy mantled pool'.

Antithesis

Antithesis is the opposition of words or phrases against each other, as when Ferdinand, discovering his father is alive, not drowned, gratefully exclaims, 'Though the seas threaten, they are merciful'.

Prospero claims that his magic has enabled him to set roaring war between sea and sky: 'the green sea and the azured vault'. This setting of word against word ('threaten' stands in opposition to 'merciful', 'green sea' to 'azured vault') is one of Shakespeare's favourite language devices. He uses it extensively in all his plays. Why? Because antithesis powerfully expresses conflict through its use of opposites, and conflict is the essence of all drama.

In *The Tempest*, conflict occurs in many forms. Characters are set against each other: Prospero versus the enemies who ousted him from Milan, Caliban versus Prospero; there is the attempted murder of Alonso by Antonio and Sebastian and the drunken Stephano's intention to kill Prospero. Ariel protests against his service, and even Ferdinand is initially treated as an enemy by Prospero.

There are all kinds of more abstract or thematic oppositions. Earth and air are set against each other, represented by Caliban and Ariel. Sebastian sneeringly compares Europe with Africa in describing the marriage of Claribel to the king of Tunis (Act 2 Scene 1, lines 118–20). Caliban contrasts Miranda with Sycorax, 'As great'st does least' (Act 3 Scene 2, lines 95–7). 'White magic' is set against 'black magic': Prospero believes his art is superior to Sycorax' malign sorcery. Two of the major themes of the play (nature–nurture, forgiveness–revenge) are expressed by Prospero in succinct antitheses: he sees Caliban as 'a born devil, on whose nature / Nurture can never stick'. Opting for mercy towards his enemies he declares, 'The rarer action is / In virtue, than in vengeance.'

Antithesis thus intensifies the sense of dramatic conflict and embodies its different forms. As the two examples given at the end of the preceding paragraph show, major themes find their linguistic expression in antitheses. But antithesis also pervades the play at all levels, making contrasts or conflicts of many different kinds as the few following examples show:

'Good wombs have borne bad sons' (Miranda, thinking of her father and his brother, Act 1 Scene 2, line 120);

'weigh / Our sorrow with our comfort' (Gonzalo, attempting to cheer Alonso, Act 2 Scene 1, lines 8–9);

'There's nothing ill can dwell in such a temple' (Miranda, defending Ferdinand, Act 1 Scene 2, line 456);

'O, she is / Ten times more gentle than her father's crabbed' (Ferdinand, comparing Miranda and Prospero, Act 3 Scene 1, lines 7–8);

'Weighed between loathness and obedience' (Sebastian, describing how Claribel was torn between her dislike of the king of Tunis and obedience to her father's wishes, Act 2 Scene 1, line 125).

Repetition

It has already been noted how the themes and actions of *The Tempest* mirror each other, for example usurpation, freedom and imprisonment, dreams and sleep. Shakespeare uses similar repetition in the language of the play. Sometimes words or phrases are repeated for particular effect: to express the fear of the sailors in the shipwreck, for example, in 'We split, we split!', or Prospero's agitation as he begins his tale of usurpation and exile, 'Twelve year since, Miranda, twelve year since'.

Different forms of language repetition run through the play, contributing to its atmosphere, creation of character, moral and political exploration, and dramatic impact. Perhaps the most obvious examples of the use of repetition are Ariel's songs and the formality of the masque. Both please the ear by being so rich in the repeated sounds of rhyme and the hypnotic effects of rhythm. But Shakespeare's skill in using repetition to heighten theatrical effect and deepen emotional and imaginative significance is evident in less obvious ways. The stateliness of Ferdinand's praise of Miranda is underlined by alliteration:

> But you, O you,
> So perfect and so peerless, are created
> Of every creature's best.   *(Act 3 Scene 1, lines 47–9)*

Repeated words, phrases, rhythms and sounds add intensity to the moment or episode, and are evident in particular speeches. A single line of Prospero's as he begins to tell his story is rich in repeated words and sounds, 'Which thou heard'st cry, which thou saw'st sink. Sit down' (Act 1 Scene 2, line 32). The repetition of the 's' sound may not have the seductive pleasure of Ariel's songs, but it enables the actor to give patterned resonance to the meaning as the echoing sibilants can help suggest the physical actions described ('sink') and demanded ('sit').

The repeated rhythms of verse are discussed below, but the play's prose also contains the same qualities of rhythmical and phrasal repetition, for example in Sebastian's and Antonio's mocking of Gonzalo in Act 2 Scene 1, and in Trinculo's soliloquy in Act 2 Scene 2. As Trinculo fears the oncoming storm and then discovers the 'strange fish' under the gaberdine, his speech has all kinds of subtle rhythmical and lexical repetitions which add to the humour, not least in the everyday 'What have we here . . . ?', still much used by comics today (note the thrice repeated 'h'), and the less familiar, but still comically alliterative 'There would this monster make a man'.

Lists

One of Shakespeare's favourite language methods is to accumulate words or phrases rather like a list. He had learned the technique ('copiousness') as a schoolboy in Stratford-upon-Avon (where different forms of the technique were given Latin names), and his skill in knowing how to use lists dramatically is evident in the many examples in *The Tempest*. He intensifies and varies description, atmosphere and argument as he 'piles up' item on item, incident on incident. For example, on his first appearance, Ariel lists his abilities: 'to fly, / To swim, to dive into the fire, to ride / On the curled clouds' (Act 1 Scene 2, lines 190–2). In the play's final scene, the Boatswain's tale of the crew's awakening is an imaginative catalogue of events and descriptions:

> We were dead of sleep,
> And – how we know not – all clapped under hatches,
> Where, but even now, with strange and several noises
> Of roaring, shrieking, howling, jingling chains,
> And more diversity of sounds, all horrible,
> We were awaked, straightway at liberty;
> Where we, in all our trim, freshly beheld
> Our royal, good, and gallant ship; our master
> Cap'ring to eye her.   *(Act 5 Scene 1, lines 230–8)*

Elsewhere, the insults and threats that Prospero and Caliban exchange or wish upon each other can be seen as Shakespeare piling up curse on curse to intensify their mutual loathing: 'I'll rack thee with old cramps, / Fill all thy bones with aches, make thee roar' (Act 1 Scene 2, lines 369–71). Shakespeare also sometimes uses very brief lists to deepen a particular mood or effect, for example 'toads, beetles, bats', 'bogs, fens, flats'.

Other speeches which you can analyse as lists (where you identify and discuss each 'element') include Ariel's story of the shipwreck (Act 1 Scene 2, lines 196–215); the story of Sycorax and Ariel (Act 1 Scene 2, lines 263–93); Caliban's tale of how he welcomed Prospero to the island (Act 1 Scene 2, lines 333–40); the threatened punishment of Ferdinand (Act 1 Scene 2, lines 460–3); Prospero's 'Our revels now are ended' speech (Act 4 Scene 1, lines 148–58); and Gonzalo's rejoicing summation of how everything has worked out for the good:

> in one voyage
> Did Claribel her husband find at Tunis,
> And Ferdinand her brother found a wife
> Where he himself was lost; Prospero, his dukedom
> In a poor isle, and all of us ourselves,
> When no man was his own.   *(Act 5 Scene 1, lines 208–13)*

The many lists in the play provide valuable opportunities for actors to vary their delivery. In speaking, a character usually seeks to give each 'item' a distinctiveness in emphasis and emotional tone, and sometimes an accompanying action and expression. In addition, the accumulating effect of lists can add to the force of argument, enrich atmosphere, amplify meaning and provide extra dimensions of character.

Verse and prose

How did Shakespeare decide whether to write in verse or prose? One answer is that he followed theatrical convention. Prose was traditionally used by comic and low-status characters. High-status characters spoke verse. 'Comic' scenes were written in prose, but audiences expected verse in 'serious' scenes: the poetic style was thought to be particularly suitable for lovers and for moments of high dramatic or emotional intensity.

Shakespeare used his judgement about which convention or principle he should follow in *The Tempest*, and it is obvious that he frequently broke the 'rules'. Caliban (very low status) speaks verse, some of it of extraordinary beauty and appeal. He uses prose in his first encounter with Stephano and Trinculo (low-status and comic characters), but ends the scene with haunting poetry as he resolves to leave Prospero and serve Stephano: 'I'll show thee the best springs; I'll pluck thee berries . . .' (Act 2 Scene 2, lines 146–58). Sebastian and Antonio (high status) use prose as they taunt Gonzalo, but thereafter use verse.

The verse of *The Tempest* is mainly blank verse: unrhymed verse written in iambic pentameter. It is conventional to define iambic pentameter as a rhythm or metre in which each line has five stressed syllables (/) alternating with five unstressed syllables (×):

× /   × / × / × / × /
So, king, go safely on to seek thy son.

At school, Shakespeare had learned the technical definition of iambic pentameter. In Greek, *penta* means 'five', and *iamb* means a 'foot' of two syllables, the first unstressed, the second stressed (as in 'alas' = aLAS). Shakespeare wrote most of his plays using this metrical pattern, and his early plays, such as *Titus Andronicus* or *Richard III*, are very regular in rhythm (often expressed as de-DUM de-DUM de-DUM de-DUM de-DUM), and with each line 'end-stopped' (making sense on its own).

By the time he came to write *The Tempest* (around 1610), Shakespeare used great variation in his verse. Very few lines are completely 'regular' (five 'beats' in order). He adds extra syllables and varies the rhythm. Many lines are not 'end-stopped', the sense running over into the following line (*enjambement*). Only in the masque are the lines consistently end-stopped (and rhyming) to emphasise the formality of the occasion. Many lines are 'shared', as a speaker ends a speech part way through a line, which is completed by the next speaker. Some critics argue that such sharing creates tension, expressing interpersonal conflicts. Others assert it conveys a sense of intimacy, resembling genuine dialogue.

Critical approaches

Traditional criticism

Early critics tended to regard *The Tempest* as a charming fantasy. They largely ignored the troubling aspects of the play. Commentators typically praised Shakespeare's imaginative creativity. In 1679 John Dryden celebrated the play's poetic invention, and singled out Caliban as remarkable in characterisation and language. Nicholas Rowe in 1709 also expressed his admiration for Shakespeare and declared the play to be 'as perfect in its kind, as almost anything we have of his'. He found Prospero's magic 'very solemn and very poetical'. Joseph Warton in 1753 gushingly delighted in playwright and play, finding *The Tempest*

> the most striking instance of his creative power. He has there given the reins to his boundless imagination, and has carried the romantic, the wonderful, and the wild, to the most pleasing extravagance . . . The poet is a more powerful magician than his own Prospero: we are transported into fairyland; we are rapt in a delicious dream.

Such views are typical of early writing about the play, seeing it as an enchanting and enchanted daydream, and its author as fancifully inspired. This stress on imaginative creativity was even more strongly emphasised by the Romantic critics of the first half of the nineteenth century. In 1811, Samuel Taylor Coleridge asserted that the play 'addresses itself entirely to the imaginative faculty'. His discussion of characters, like that of his critical predecessors, continued to use the same flowery language. Ariel is 'like a May-blossom kept suspended in the air by the fanning breeze'.

In contrast to earlier critics, Coleridge discovered deeper significances in Caliban, finding him 'in some respects a noble being: the poet has raised him far above contempt'. But the unqualified praise of Shakespeare's 'might and majesty of genius' continued: 'from his astonishing and intuitive knowledge of what man must be at all times, and under all circumstances, he is rather to be looked upon as a prophet than as a poet'. For the Romantics, Prospero came to resemble Shakespeare himself.

William Hazlitt was similarly fulsome in 1817: '*The Tempest* is one of the most original and perfect of Shakespeare's productions . . . full of grace and grandeur.' But like Coleridge, Hazlitt was also concerned to alter the traditional perception of Caliban as no more than a savage or buffoon: Caliban's 'deformity whether of body or mind is redeemed by the power and truth of the imagination displayed in it'. Like his fellow Romantics, Hazlitt was impressed by what they saw as the truth and harmony in Shakespeare's artistic design. They regarded the play as a dramatic poem expressing Shakespeare's poetic vision. Such judgements were derived from their reading of the play. What they saw staged were not versions of Shakespeare's original but radical adaptations of it (see pages 101–3). Hazlitt was outraged by an extravagantly spectacular production he saw (see page 102) and Charles Lamb was tartly sceptical of the value of stage performance, declaring his preference for reading the play rather than watching it in the theatre:

> It is one thing to read of an enchanter, and to believe the wondrous tale while we are reading it; but to have a conjurer brought before us in his conjuring-gown, with his spirits about him, which none but himself and some hundred of favoured spectators before the curtain are supposed to see, involves such a quantity of the hateful incredible, that all our reverence for the author cannot hinder us from perceiving such gross attempts upon the senses to be in the highest degree childish and inefficient.

The Romantics were alert to some of the troubling aspects of the play, and 'stood up' for Caliban. Nevertheless, as the nineteenth century progressed, a sentimental concentration on character became pronounced, and the desire to equate Shakespeare with Prospero intensified. Edward Dowden in a significantly entitled essay, 'The serenity of *The Tempest*' (1875), is typical in regarding the play as an unproblematic product of a contented, ageing Shakespeare, retiring to Stratford-upon-Avon and bidding farewell to the stage in the character of Prospero. The Epilogue is seen as Shakespeare 'passing from his service as artist to his service as English country gentleman'. Judgements which today are regarded as quite inappropriate are made about character and author:

> We identify Prospero in some measure with Shakespeare himself . . . the grave harmony of his character, his self-mastery, his calm validity of will, his sensitivity to wrong, his unfaltering justice.

Most traditional criticism of *The Tempest* is preoccupied with character. Modern criticism is uneasy about discussing characters in this way, preferring to see them as fictional creations in a stage drama. However, it would be inappropriate to think of traditional criticism as concerned solely with character. All kinds of different approaches exist within it. Before discussing particular critics it is helpful to note that many have remarked on how *The Tempest* 'observes the unities'. The 'unities' is a well-known theory of drama (based partly, but not entirely accurately, on the writings of the Greek philosopher Aristotle) which states that, if a play is to possess aesthetic harmony, it must observe the unities of action, time and place. This means that it should have a single action lasting less than 24 hours, enacted in a single location. *The Tempest* is unlike all of Shakespeare's other plays, with the exception of *The Comedy of Errors*, in that it does just that:

- *Time* The action of the play takes place in under four hours (see Act 1 Scene 2, lines 239–41, and Act 5 Scene 1, lines 186 and 223).
- *Place* Apart from the opening shipwreck scene, everything takes place on the island.
- *Action* All the sub-plots link neatly to the central plot of the usurpation of Prospero and his plan to regain his dukedom.

G Wilson Knight (1947) considers *The Tempest* in the context of all Shakespeare's plays: '*The Tempest*, patterned of storm and music, is thus an interpretation of Shakespeare's world.' Knight considers the play's characters and events in turn, and in each finds echoes of Shakespeare's earlier creations. For example 'The faithful and garrulous old lord Gonzalo' is a blend of Polonius (*Hamlet*), Adam (*As You Like It*) and Kent (*King Lear*). Knight finds in other plays precedents for, and parallels to, the banquet, the comic scenes, the hunting of the murderous conspirators, their drunkenness, and even the stagnant water into which they are led. Knight's argument is that *The Tempest* and the other 'late plays' express Shakespeare's deepest concerns, and distil his life's work. But Knight's desire (like so many before him) to find Shakespeare in *The Tempest* topples into purple-prose absurdity when he adds together the 12 years Ariel suffers captivity and the 12 years Prospero has spent on the island to find that this was

> roughly the time spent by Shakespeare in his earlier work, before the powers of bitterness and abysmal sight projected him into the twilit, lightning-riven and finally transcendent regions.

E M W Tillyard (1954) considered *The Tempest*'s relationship to Shakespeare's other 'late plays', seeing all as directed towards the achievement of order and happiness. He detects a 'tragic pattern' in *The Tempest*, with Prospero as a king who makes a tragic mistake, but who experiences regeneration through suffering. The 'tragic element' (the deposition of Prospero) is told rather than shown. Tillyard argues that Prospero does not change fundamentally through the play, as many critics claim, but is inclined to mercy from the start. The traditional view is that Prospero seeks revenge on Alonso, but Tillyard claims that the fact that Prospero prevents Antonio and Sebastian from murdering his old enemy 'is proof of his already achieved regeneration from vengeance to mercy'.

One critic goes even further in her challenge to see the play in its relationship to Shakespeare's other works. Rose Abdelnour Zimbardo (1968) asserts that critics are 'completely in error' in attempting to interpret *The Tempest* in light of other plays, or to see it as about regeneration. She uses a different, but still traditional perspective, claiming 'the heart of the play is not regeneration through suffering but the eternal conflict between order and chaos'. For Zimbardo, Prospero is an artist who controls through his art. He finds himself up against wicked characters who are not obedient to the laws of political or emotional order, but Prospero himself has 'order' always firmly in mind, and his project in raising the tempest that sinks Alonso's ship is to cure the disorder in others, and to bring about social order through the marriage of Ferdinand and Miranda.

Caroline Spurgeon (1935) opened up a further critical perspective on *The Tempest*: the study of its imagery. In *Shakespeare's Imagery and What It Tells Us*, Spurgeon identifies patterns of imagery in each of

Shakespeare's plays. She finds that the dominant image of *The Tempest* is expressed through the action and background of the play:

> It is the sense of sound which is thus emphasised, for the play itself is an absolute symphony of sound . . . the singing of the winds and the roaring of the waters, the cries of the drowning men, the reverberation of the thunder . . . chattering apes and hissing adders, the drunken shouts and catches of Caliban and his companions . . . the owl's cry, the cock's crow and the dog's bark . . . the humming of 'a thousand twangling instruments' . . . the contrast of sweet songs and airs, delicate and bewitching . . . and through it all the continually recurrent strains of music.

Although the value of Caroline Spurgeon's pioneering study of Shakespeare's imagery has been acknowledged by later critics, her work has also been much criticised. She only occasionally examines how the imagery relates to the dramatic context of the play, makes no mention of sexual imagery, and insistently and repeatedly claims that her method gives direct access to Shakespeare's own thoughts, feelings, nature and experience. For example when Prospero remarks that his 'enemies are all knit up in their distractions' she claims it shows 'knitting he [Shakespeare] has often watched'.

One of the best-known interpretations in traditional criticism is that of Frank Kermode (1968). He sees *The Tempest* as a pastoral play centrally concerned with the theme of Nature and Art. Here 'Art' means all the ways in which human beings, in pursuit of a moral, civilised life, try to improve on Nature. Kermode sees Prospero's 'art' as 'a beneficent magic' designed to achieve that goal: 'Prospero is, therefore, the representative of Art, as Caliban is of Nature'. Prospero uses his learning to control for good purposes, unlike Sycorax who uses her powers to achieve evil ends. In the same vein, Kermode contrasts Ferdinand and Miranda with Caliban: they possess nobility, he does not. Kermode sees in Antonio and Sebastian how unnatural vices may corrupt nobility. He argues that *The Tempest* resembles the pastoral tradition in opposing civilised and sophisticated values with 'primitive' existence. His essay draws upon travellers' tales (discussed on page 75) to illustrate that opposition, and incidently demonstrates that 'colonialism' is not simply a very recent concern of criticism:

These apparently antithetical views on the natural life to some extent controlled the reports of the voyagers upon whom Montaigne and Shakespeare both depend. They tended to describe the natives as purely virtuous or purely vicious . . . they repeat the theme of Montaigne's commonwealth; and yet they also speak of the brutality of the natives, of their treachery, ugliness, and infidelity . . . Behind all these observations are the two opposing versions of the natural; on the one hand, that which man corrupts, and on the other that which is defective, and must be mended by cultivation – the less than human, which calls forth man's authoritative power to correct and rule. This latter is the view which suits best the conscience of the colonist.

Kermode's view of the play as being about 'Nature and Art' is obviously a thematic approach, which offers one kind of answer to the question 'What is the play about?' by identifying its major preoccupations as abstractions or themes. Many other critics have identified what they see as the themes of the play. Throughout this Guide you can find numerous examples of those themes: usurpation, colonialism, forgiveness and reconciliation, justice and mercy, imprisonment and freedom, magic and illusion, change, time and fate, music, sleep and dreams, discovery and wonder, memory.

Modern criticism

Throughout the second half of the twentieth century and in the twenty-first, critical approaches to Shakespeare have radically challenged the style and assumptions of the traditional approaches described above. New critical approaches argue that traditional interpretations, often heavily focused on character, are individualistic and misleading. The traditional concentration on personal feelings ignores society and history, and so divorces literary, dramatic and aesthetic matters from their social context. Further, their detachment from the real world makes them elitist, sexist and unpolitical.

Modern critical perspectives therefore shift the focus from individuals to how social conditions (of the world of the play and of Shakespeare's England) are reflected in characters' relationships, language and behaviour. Modern criticism also concerns itself with how social assumptions and practices at different periods right up to the present have affected interpretations of the play. In this regard, *The Tempest* has probably attracted more radical critical attention than almost any other of Shakespeare's plays. Modern critics have identified and explored its troubling ambivalences and ambiguities and, in particular, placed it in the context of centuries of colonialism. In short, the play has frequently been used as a critical test-bed for new critical theories of approaches to drama and literature.

This section will explore how recent critical approaches to Shakespeare have been used to address *The Tempest*. Like traditional criticism, contemporary perspectives include many different approaches but share common features. Modern criticism:

- is sceptical of 'character' approaches (but often uses them);
- concentrates on political, social and economic factors (arguing that these factors determine Shakespeare's creativity and audiences' and critics' interpretations);
- identifies contradictions, fragmentation and disunity in the plays;
- questions the possibility of 'happy' or 'hopeful' endings, preferring ambiguous, unsettling or sombre endings;
- produces readings that are subversive of existing social structures;
- identifies how the plays express the interests of dominant groups, particularly rich and powerful males;
- insists that 'theory' (psychological, social, etc.) is essential to produce valid readings;
- often expresses its commitment (for example, to feminism, or equality, or anti-colonialism, or political change);
- argues that all readings are political or ideological readings (and that traditional criticism falsely claims to be objective);
- argues that traditional approaches have always interpreted Shakespeare conservatively, in ways that confirm and maintain the interests of the elite or dominant class.

The following discussion is organised under headings which represent major contemporary critical perspectives on *The Tempest* (political, postcolonial, feminist, performance, psychoanalytic, postmodern). But it is vital to appreciate that there is often overlap between the categories, and that to pigeonhole any example of criticism too precisely is to reduce its value and application. Any single critical essay may have a dominant focus, but it usually takes account of other approaches.

Political criticism

'Political criticism' is a convenient label for approaches concerned with power and social structure: in the world of the play, in Shakespeare's time and in our own. Throughout *The Tempest*, power is repeatedly contested: the Boatswain orders away the king and courtiers; Prospero tells of his overthrow as Duke of Milan; both Ariel and Caliban protest about their servitude; Stephano intends to take over the island; even Miranda ventures a protest against Prospero on Ferdinand's behalf. Simply to list these few examples of the multiple challenges to power in the play reveals the problem of 'classification' noted in the preceding paragraph, because they include political, anti-colonial and gender contestations of authority. However, as modern criticism of *The Tempest* tends to be grouped under political, postcolonial and feminist approaches, this Guide will reflect those subdivisions. This discussion of 'political criticism' will therefore largely confine itself to questions of government and usurpation, the overthrow of a ruler. But the most obvious political question of state, 'Who has the right to own and rule the island?', will be discussed under 'Postcolonial criticism' below.

Political critics have tended to concentrate on Prospero's usurpation by his brother Antonio. They show how that overthrow is reflected in the various usurpation attempts in the play, most notably, as a matter of state, the planned but unsuccessful attempt on the life of King Alonso. Here, Stephen Greenblatt (1988) uses the 1610 Strachey letter (see page 66) for its detail of the two rebellions against the shipwrecked governor on Bermuda, and the later imposition of strict military discipline upon the potentially mutinous settlers in Jamestown, Virginia. In the first island rebellion, the leader was pardoned; in the second, the rebel was summarily executed. Greenblatt sees Shakespeare deliberately appropriating such material to convey both 'the powerful social energy of princely pardons' (a common practice of sixteenth- and seventeenth-century monarchs), and how 'a triumphant affirmation of absolute control' can be achieved in the face of a 'crisis in authority provoked by both danger and excess, a fear of lower-class disorder and upper-class ambition'. In the play these become Prospero pardoning his enemies, and the 'revolts' of Caliban and Stephano, Antonio and Sebastian.

Other political critics have argued that the play gives voice to oppositional, republican sentiments. Here, Gonzalo's 'commonwealth' speech has been interpreted as communist and anarchic, an idealised utopia. Such critics detect the language of radical utopianism permeating the play, which gives a voice to alternative political systems to one based on traditional monarchy.

A well-known critic who is often called upon in support of political interpretations of Shakespeare's plays is the Polish scholar Jan Kott. Kott fought with the Polish army and underground movement against the Nazis in the Second World War (1939–45) and had direct experience of the suffering and terror caused by Stalinist repression in Poland in the years after the war. Kott's book *Shakespeare Our Contemporary* (1965) saw parallels between the violence and cruelty of the modern world and the worlds of tyranny and despair that Shakespeare depicted in his tragedies. His discussion of *The Tempest* is similarly concerned to show how it reflects modern political cynicism, violence, conflict and social breakdown. Kott places much weight on Gonzalo's apprehensive description of the island:

> All torment, trouble, wonder, and amazement
> Inhabits here. Some heavenly power guide us
> Out of this fearful country!   *(Act 5 Scene 1, lines 104–6)*

Kott recognises the island is no utopia: 'on Prospero's island the laws of the real world apply', and Kott sees that world as relentlessly cruel, violent and oppressive. The dark political setting is revealed in the story Prospero tells of his usurpation: 'Prospero's narrative is a description of a struggle for power, of violence and conspiracy'. Kott's acknowledgement that it is repeated in the story of Ariel and Caliban leads him to assert that 'violence, as the principle on which the world is based, will be shown in cosmic terms'. Kott argues that on the island, Shakespeare's history of the world is played out, and 'History itself is madness', consisting in Kott's view of a violent and murderous struggle for power.

Postcolonial criticism

'Postcolonial criticism' has gathered increasing pace (and its label) from the 1980s, but it existed in different forms well before then. In the second half of the twentieth century, Great Britain and other European states experienced the disintegration of their empires as former colonies gained independence and became fully fledged nation states. In India, Africa and the Caribbean, countries whose native inhabitants had long echoed Caliban's protest 'This island's mine' at last shook off the domination of their European rulers.

Under such conditions, the appeal of *The Tempest* is evident, both before independence as a vehicle of protest, and afterwards as an artistic medium through which to examine the experience of colonisation. Many African and Caribbean writers have used the play and its central symbols as allegories of colonialist relationships. For example, in the 1930s, Aimé Césalre (born in 1913 in Martinique, then a French colony) rewrote the play from Caliban's viewpoint as *Une Tempête*. His play portrayed the plight of African slaves on Martinique and their struggle against the slave-owning Prospero. George Lamming's Caribbean novel *Water with Berries* (1972) uses the Prospero–Caliban theme. But the book which has heavily influenced criticism (and stage interpretations) is an anthropological text written by a French colonial official: Octave Mannoni's *Prospero and Caliban*. Published in English in 1956 (it first appeared in French in 1950 as *Psychologie de la colonisation*), it gave a detailed account of the behaviour of the French colonists of Madagascar and the reaction of the indigenous population. It recorded a picture of brutal, callous and neurotic oppressors and submissive, resentful natives. Most postcolonial critics acknowledge their debt to Mannoni's pioneering work in recording the bitter legacy of colonisation.

Pages 72–5 have discussed the impact of European colonisation on the 'New World' of the Americas. That experience has been used by postcolonial critics to expose the brutality which lies behind Prospero's apparent denial that culture existed before he came to the island, and his belief that Caliban was, and is, no more than an animal. Such critics have pointed out that much traditional criticism assumed, often without discussion, Prospero's right to take ownership of the island. Some argue that the play is complicit in the mythology of benevolent colonialism: that the benefits Prospero brings justifies his seizure of the island and enslavement of Caliban. Just as the colonising Europeans of the sixteenth and seventeenth centuries felt that what they took to be their superior knowledge, sophistication and religion justified their colonisation (typically by superior force), so too does Prospero.

The majority of postcolonial critics argue that the play contains its own implicit questioning of the legitimacy of colonisation or the inferiority of native inhabitants. To give only one example, they point to the fact that Shakespeare gives Caliban the most eloquent, and perhaps the most moving speech in the play, 'Be not afeared, the isle is full of noises' (Act 3 Scene 2, lines 130–8). Prospero and Miranda may have taught him to know how to curse, but he also possesses the most haunting voice in the play.

'Seizing the Book' by the Indian critic Ania Loomba gathers together many of the key issues in postcolonial criticism. She shows how, in the text, in its staging and criticism, and in the institutions in which it is taught, colonialist implications of class, gender, race, caste and ethnicity all intersect. She is critical of influential criticism such as that of Frank Kermode's (see page 92) which, by foregrounding such themes as 'the opposition of Nature and Art', marginalise or 'background' the colonialist, 'New World' material which sparked Shakespeare's imagination. In her own experience (Loomba was educated in India), such criticism turns students' attention to 'the Romance tradition' or to 'forgiveness, patience and magic', rather than to the lived experience of the colonised peoples, or to the fictionalised, dramatic experience of Caliban himself. She shows how *The Tempest* was (and is) used to encourage Indian readers to identify with the coloniser rather than with the colonised: 'closer to noble, white Prospero than monstrous black Caliban'. Such criticism and teaching erases the imperial theme, but for the postcolonial critic they underline the colonial history of the play.

Loomba argues that conservative and radical criticism alike has constructed 'the colonial subject' in such a way that Caliban 'does not threaten commonsense notions about black people or slaves'. Rather, it confirms that stereotyped image of brutal savages, and upholds the myth of the black man as potential rapist. Similarly, Loomba criticises stage portrayals that present Caliban as animal-like and deformed as 'explicitly social-Darwinist, racist and imperialist productions'. Loomba makes clear the central assumption of postcolonial criticism:

> Prospero's takeover is both racial plunder and a transfer to patriarchy . . . Prospero as colonialist consolidates power that

is specifically white and male, and constructs Sycorax as a black, wayward and wicked witch in order to legitimise it.

Modern stagings have often employed postcolonial criticism to inform their interpretations. A well-known example is Dr Jonathan Miller's 1970 production presenting the play as a story of colonial oppression. The interpretation was in sharp contrast to the traditional image of Prospero as a benevolent ruler. Miller was heavily influenced by Mannoni's book (see page 97) and saw the play as 'the tragic and inevitable disintegration of more primitive culture as the result of European invasion and colonisation'. He compared Stephano and Trinculo to foreign soldiers who patronise and bully the native population, 'they shout loudly at the people to make them understand, make them drunk and get drunk themselves'. Caliban was 'the demoralised, detribalised, dispossessed, suffering field-hand'.

Feminist criticism

Feminism aims to achieve rights and equality for women in social, political and economic life. It challenges sexism: those beliefs and practices which result in the degradation, oppression and subordination of women. Feminist critics therefore reject 'male ownership' of criticism in which men determined what questions were to be asked of a play and which answers were acceptable. They argue that male criticism often neglects, represses or misrepresents female experience and stereotypes or distorts women's points of view.

At first sight, *The Tempest* seems to offer only limited prospects for feminist interpretations. Women are notable by their absence. There are few female characters who appear and speak. Miranda seems to live in a system under her father's domination (patriarchy), and has only a faint recollection of the four or five women who attended her in infancy. Her mother is only once mentioned, and that briefly by Prospero; Miranda does not ask about her. The goddesses Iris, Ceres and Juno make just one appearance in the masque (and are played by Ariel and his spirits). Ferdinand's mother is never mentioned, and his sister Claribel's absence is stressed: 'she that dwells / Ten leagues beyond man's life'. Caliban's mother is long dead; reviled as a 'foul witch', she was earlier banished from Algiers to the island. With facts like these in mind, Ann Thompson (1999) asks a key question:

I want to ask what feminist criticism can do in the face of a male-authored canonical text which seems to exclude women to this extent.

Clearly, one major feminist approach seems unavailable: that which focuses on the strength of female characters and how they challenge or subvert male domination. Thompson reports her students' response to Miranda (who Prospero contemptuously calls 'my foot'). They think her 'an extremely feeble heroine and scorn to identify with her'. She seems to give little scope for a feminist approach, and Thompson notes how nineteenth-century writers stressed her 'modesty, grace and tenderness'. Thompson offers her own modern comment that 'Miranda demonstrates that she has fully internalised the patriarchal assumption that a woman's main function is to provide a legitimate succession' when she remarks about Antonio that 'Good wombs have borne bad sons.'

Such thoughts lead Thompson to argue that something other than a character approach must therefore be used; that could be an attempt 'to explore the "ideology of femininity" at work in *The Tempest*' by focusing on issues of gender, on how female sexuality functions in the play. She points first to the fact that Miranda is crucial to the play: Prospero tells her about the storm he has raised, 'I have done nothing but in care of thee'. But Thompson's major concern is to demonstrate how the play's imagery and events are obsessed with the themes of chastity and fertility. It is helpful to list some of the very different ways in which this female-centred preoccupation is expressed:

- Gonzalo remarks that the ship is as leaky as 'an unstanched wench': a sexually aroused or menstruating woman.
- Prospero seems to claim he gave second birth to Miranda on the voyage to the island: 'Under my burden groaned'.
- The virginal Miranda is contrasted with the 'earthy and abhorred' Sycorax, who, according to Prospero, had sex with the Devil to conceive Caliban.
- Caliban as would-be rapist, and later virtually a pimp to Stephano, promises him Miranda as a sexual prize.
- Ferdinand asks on first seeing Miranda, 'If you be maid, or no?' and expresses concern that she should be 'a virgin' to become Queen of Naples.

- Prospero repeatedly warns Ferdinand against pre-marital sex.
- The masque explicitly banishes lust in the form of Venus and Cupid.
- Birth or rebirth is parodied in such images as 'sea-swallowed though some cast again' and 'never-surfeited sea / Hath caused to belch you up'.

Thompson asks how a feminist can interpret this pattern of references which attributes enormous power to female chastity and fertility. Her response identifies features much concerned with male control: the fathers, Prospero and Alonso, control their daughters' sexuality; males control the fertility of nature (Ceres is played by Ariel); the stresses that arise in attempts to exercise patriarchal control. Thompson argues for exploring the gaps and blanks Shakespeare leaves, for example attention to absent wives and mothers (this can resemble a psychoanalytic approach, see pages 104–5), and an exploration of the network of feminine allusions throughout the text, for example the implications of Gonzalo referring to Dido as 'widow', discussed on page 18.

Performance criticism

Performance criticism fully acknowledges that *The Tempest* is a play: a script to be performed by actors to an audience. It examines all aspects of the play in performance: its staging in the theatre or on film and video. Performance criticism focuses on Shakespeare's stagecraft and the semiotics of theatre (signs: words, costumes, gestures, etc.), together with the 'afterlife' of the play (what happened to *The Tempest* after Shakespeare wrote it). That involves scrutiny of how productions at different periods have presented the play. As such, performance criticism appraises how the text has been cut, added to, rewritten and rearranged to present a version felt appropriate to the times (see Dymkowski in the Resources section, page 125).

Only two performances of the play are known for certain to have taken place in Shakespeare's lifetime, both at the court of King James I, in 1611 and 1613. Many scholars believe, however, that the play would have also been performed at the Blackfriars and the Globe, the two playhouses owned by Shakespeare's acting company, the King's Men.

The Tempest has always been extremely popular on stage, but for over 200 years the version performed was not the one that

Shakespeare wrote. In 1667, the play was rewritten by William Davenant and John Dryden as *The Enchanted Island*. Only one-third of Shakespeare's play was included and a great deal was added. Davenant considered he was 'purifying' Shakespeare, removing whatever was considered rough or coarse, and adding and revising to produce a play that satisfied the current neoclassical standards expected of any art form. Caliban and Miranda were given sisters. A male character appeared, Hippolito, Duke of Mantua. He had never seen a woman, and was under a curse that he would die if he ever did see one. The masque and the role of Sebastian were left out entirely, and much more comedy, dance and music was inserted. Caliban was merely a comic figure. The politics and sexuality of Shakespeare's play became much less sharp-edged. The adaptation proved very popular; the diarist Samuel Pepys saw it five times in four months, reporting that it 'still pleases me mightily'.

In 1674, Davenant's and Dryden's version was adapted as an opera by Thomas Shadwell (who provided Ariel with a girlfriend), and performances became increasingly concerned with theatrical spectacle. Expensive stage machinery created spectacular effects, particularly in the storm scene and in the flying of Ariel and the other spirits. This version of *The Tempest* was revived in many adaptations during the eighteenth and nineteenth centuries (and is claimed to be one of the inspirations for English pantomime), with every production aiming at enthralling theatrical extravaganza. One version shifted the storm scene to the start of Act 2 so that late-comers to the theatre would not miss the elaborate stage effects. Another version contained 32 songs.

These operatic and balletic versions of *The Tempest* attracted large audiences, but were often criticised for being more like pantomimes. In 1815, the critic William Hazlitt was outraged by what he saw, calling it 'travesty, caricature . . . vulgar and ridiculous . . . clap-trap sentiments . . . heavy tinsel and affected formality'. He declared himself tempted never again to see a Shakespeare play (a temptation he immediately resisted).

Notwithstanding such criticism, the spectacular version of *The Tempest* proved popular with audiences. Each new production was hugely successful and very profitable. In spite of an attempt by David Garrick in the period 1757–76, it was not until towards the middle of the nineteenth century that serious efforts were made to present the play as Shakespeare had written it. W C Macready's 1838 production used Shakespeare's text, but retained some of Ariel's songs from the operatic version. Subsequent Victorian productions still employed lavish special effects (an 1857 production required 140 stagehands). Miranda continued to be played as a sweet innocent (her 'Abhorrèd slave' speech cut or given to Prospero).

Perhaps most significantly, Caliban, previously depicted as a clownish figure of fun, began to be played as a degraded slave, so evoking the audience's pity. From the time of that Victorian portrayal, the comic aspects of Caliban were increasingly balanced by more serious concerns. In 1904 Sir Herbert Beerbohm Tree brought out Caliban's sensitivity and potential nobility. In late twentieth century and early twenty-first century productions, colonialist and anti-imperial approaches to the play have become common. The earlier benign portrayals of Prospero yielded to more complex character-isation: brooding, irritable, vengeful, harsh. Questions of power and gender discussed in modern criticism have increasingly affected contemporary productions.

Although the elaborate scenic effects of the eighteenth and nineteenth centuries were gradually abandoned, the nature of the play seems to invite theatrical invention. Some 'bare stage' productions have been performed (beginning with William Poel's 1897 scenery-less production), but many if not most professional productions try to capture the magic and wonder the play expresses. For example, the 2002 Royal Shakespeare Company version used elaborate machinery to stage the shipwreck, and contained striking examples of dramatic illusion (Ariel as a harpy emerged from a beheaded swan). Many modern directors feel free to adapt the text as their artistic interpretations guide them, perhaps most famously in Peter Brook's 1968 deliberately fractured and disturbing production which heavily emphasised the sexual and rebellious aspects of the play (Ferdinand and Miranda have sex, an action parodied by other characters; Caliban rapes Miranda and takes over the island).

Today most stage productions of *The Tempest* make only minor changes to Shakespeare's text and try to avoid the sentimental escapism of earlier versions. Instead, they take the opportunities that Shakespeare provides in abundance to explore the many ambiguities and conflicts that exist in the script. Sexual tensions are explored (or created), for example as productions suggest erotic relationships between Prospero and Miranda or Ariel, and between Miranda and Ferdinand or Caliban. Increasingly, throughout the twentieth century interpretations and productions of *The Tempest* have stressed the contrasts and conflicts between Prospero and Caliban, between colonist and native inhabitant (as in Jonathan Miller's production discussed on page 99).

Psychoanalytic criticism

In the twentieth century, psychoanalysis became a major influence on the understanding and interpretation of human behaviour. The founder of psychoanalysis, Sigmund Freud, explained personality as the result of unconscious and irrational desires, repressed memories or wishes, sexuality, fantasy, anxiety and conflict. Freud's theories have had a strong influence on criticism and stagings of Shakespeare's plays, most famously on *Hamlet* in the well-known claim that Hamlet suffers from an Oedipus complex.

The ambivalences and ambiguities of *The Tempest*, and its intense and fraught family relationships, have prompted much attention from critics who adopt a psychoanalytic approach to Shakespeare's plays. The gaps and blanks which Shakespeare leaves in the text have been addressed with enthusiasm and imagination as revealing 'the textual unconscious'. Different studies have concentrated on anxieties about absent mothers, or on sibling rivalry (the brothers Prospero and Antonio, Alonso and Sebastian). A focus on sexual anxieties produces very non-traditional readings: Prospero has been interpreted as harbouring incestuous desires for Miranda, and as using her as 'sexual bait' to justify his enslavement of Caliban. The 'sun-burned sicklemen' who appear in the masque have been interpreted as implying castration.

The Freudian notion of 'dreamwork' (dreams reveal unconscious wishes) has been employed both as an analogy for artistic creation and fantasy and to argue that Prospero imposes his memory of past events on Ariel and Caliban. The concept of 'wish fulfilment' has led some critics to argue that Prospero's wishes are imperfectly fulfilled, and he ends the play alone, sexually and socially. Other psychoanalytic interpretations have seen Milan as a mother that Antonio usurps; fantasies of rape in Ferdinand's speech 'the murkiest den, / The most oppòrtune place . . .' (Act 4 Scene 1, lines 25–8); and the play as having links with Shakespeare's own family life.

Such interpretations reveal the obvious weaknesses in applying psychoanalytic theories to *The Tempest*. They cannot be proved or disproved, and they are highly speculative. Psychoanalytic approaches are therefore often accused of imposing interpretations based on theory rather than upon Shakespeare's text. But the play's evident interest in troubled family relationships and in fantasy, dreams and illusions suggest why some critics discuss it as a psychiatric case history, and employ psychoanalytic concepts in their interpretations.

Ruth Nevo's assumption typifies psychoanalytic approaches: '*The Tempest* invites reflection upon the relationship between Freud and Shakespeare at a number of points of convergence'. She finds 'the animating fantasy of *The Tempest* is itself embedded in Prospero's name: it is a grand design for happiness snatched out of disaster'. The play is Prospero's 'daydream', 'a journey into a psychic interior', and his magicianship is 'the secondary organising fantasy, a fantasy of omnipotence'. Discussing Sycorax and her relationships with Ariel and Caliban, Nevo sees Prospero as 'replacing the bad mother, he is a father to them both, scolding, castigating, punishing, teaching'.

Nevo warns against over-precise application of Freudian concepts to *The Tempest*. She is critical of those who use the psychoanalytic theory that human personality is made up of ego, id and superego (reason that controls, libidinous lust and desire that drives, and conscience that restrains). To try to equate these three dimensions of personality with Prospero, Caliban and Ariel respectively is superficially appealing, but misleading.

Postmodern criticism

Postmodern criticism (sometimes called 'deconstruction' or 'post-structuralism') is often difficult to understand because it is not centrally concerned with consistency or reasoned argument. It does not accept that one section of the story is necessarily connected to what follows, or that characters relate to each other in meaningful ways. Because of such assumptions, postmodern criticism is sometimes described as 'reading against the grain' or less politely as 'textual harassment'. The approach therefore has obvious drawbacks in providing a model for examination students who are expected to display reasoned, coherent argument, and respect for the evidence of the text.

Postmodern approaches to *The Tempest* are most clearly seen in stage productions. There, you could think of it as simply 'a mixture of styles'. The label 'postmodern' is applied to productions which selfconsciously show little regard for consistency in character, or for coherence in telling the story. Characters are dressed in costumes from very different historical periods. Ironically, Shakespeare himself has been regarded as a postmodern writer in the way he mixes genres in his plays, comedy with tragedy and romance.

Some critics focus on minor or marginal characters, or on gaps or silences in the play. They claim that these features, previously overlooked as unimportant, reveal significant truths about the play. But postmodern criticism most typically revels in the cleverness of its own use of language, and accepts all kinds of anomalies and contradictions in a spirit of playfulness or 'carnival'. It abandons any notion of the organic unity of the play, and rejects the assumption that a Shakespeare play possesses clear patterns or themes. Some postmodern critics even deny the possibility of finding meaning in language. They claim that words simply refer to other words, and so any interpretation is endlessly delayed (or 'deferred' as the deconstructionists say).

Such postmodern critics make much of what they call 'the instability of language'. In practice this often means little more than traditional notions of ambiguity: that words can have different meanings. It has long been accepted that Shakespeare's language has multiple, not single meanings. The essay by Francis Barker and Peter Hulme (1999) uses the language and concepts of post-structuralist theory (but is much concerned with postcolonial criticism's warning that Prospero's viewpoint is untrustworthy). Their final comment gives an indication of post-structuralism's demanding style and its central concern with language ('discursive con-texts', 'discursive formations'):

> We have been concerned to show how *The Tempest* has been severed from its discursive con-texts through being produced by criticism as an autotelic unity, and we have tried therefore to exemplify an approach that would engage with the fully dialectical relationship between the detail of the text and the larger discursive formations.

Organising your responses

The purpose of this section is to help you improve your writing about *The Tempest*. It offers practical guidance on two kinds of tasks: writing about an extract from the play and writing an essay. Whether you are answering an examination question, preparing coursework (term papers), or carrying out research into your own chosen topic, this section will help you organise and present your responses.

In all your writing, there are three vital things to remember:

- *The Tempest* is a play. Although it is usually referred to as a 'text', *The Tempest* is not a book, but a script intended to be acted on a stage. So your writing should demonstrate an awareness of the play in performance as theatre. That means you should always try to read the play with an 'inner eye', thinking about how it could look and sound on stage. The next best thing to seeing an actual production is to imagine yourself sitting in the audience, watching and listening to *The Tempest* being performed. By doing so, you will be able to write effectively about Shakespeare's language and dramatic techniques.

- *The Tempest* is not a presentation of 'reality'. It is a dramatic construct in which the playwright, through theatre, engages the emotions and intellect of the audience. The characters and story may persuade an audience to suspend its disbelief for several hours. The audience may identify with the characters, be deeply moved by them, and may think of them as if they are living human beings. However, when you write, a major part of your task is to show how Shakespeare achieves his dramatic effects that so engage the audience. Through discussion of his handling of language, character and plot, your writing reveals how Shakespeare uses themes and ideas, attitudes and values, to give insight into crucial social, moral and political dilemmas of his time – and yours.

- How Shakespeare learned his craft. As a schoolboy, and in his early years as a dramatist, Shakespeare used all kinds of models or frameworks to guide his writing. But he quickly learned how to vary and adapt the models to his own dramatic purposes. This section offers frameworks that you can use to structure your writing. As you use them, follow Shakespeare's example! Adapt them to suit your own writing style and needs.

Writing about an extract

It is an expected part of all Shakespeare study that you should be able to write well about an extract (sometimes called a 'passage') from the play. An extract is usually between 30 and 70 lines long, and you are invited to comment on it. The instructions vary. Sometimes the task is very briefly expressed:

- Write a detailed commentary on the following passage.
- Write about the effect of the extract on your own thoughts and feelings.

At other times a particular focus is specified for your writing:

- With close reference to the language and imagery of the passage, show in what ways it helps to establish important issues in the play.
- Analyse the style and structure of the extract, showing what it contributes to your appreciation of the play's major concerns.

In writing your response, you must of course take account of the precise wording of the task, and ensure you concentrate on each particular point specified. But however the invitation to write about an extract is expressed, it requires you to comment in detail on the language. You should identify and evaluate how the language reveals character, contributes to plot development, offers opportunities for dramatic effect, and embodies crucial concerns of the play as a whole. These 'crucial concerns' are also referred to as the 'themes', or 'issues', or 'preoccupations' of the play.

The following framework is a guide to how you can write a detailed commentary on an extract. Writing a paragraph or more on each item will help you bring out the meaning and significance of the extract, and show how Shakespeare achieves his effects.

> **Paragraph 1:** Locate the extract in the play and say who is on stage.
> **Paragraph 2:** State what the extract is about and identify its structure.
> **Paragraph 3:** Identify the mood or atmosphere of the extract.
> **Paragraphs 4–8:**   These paragraphs analyse how
> Diction (vocabulary)   Shakespeare achieves his effects. They
> Imagery   concentrate on the language of the
> Antithesis   extract, showing the dramatic effect of
> Repetition   each item, and how the language
> Lists   expresses crucial concerns of the play.
> **Paragraph 9:** Staging opportunities
> **Paragraph 10:** Conclusion

The analysis and examples of different types of language used in this Guide (imagery, antithesis, etc., see pages 79–87) will help you in constructing your own response.

The following example uses the framework to show how the paragraphs making up the essay might be written. The framework headings (in bold) would not of course appear in your essay. They are presented only to help you see how the framework is used. The extract is from Act 5 Scene 1, lines 1–57 (you may also find it helpful to read how the passage is discussed in the commentary, pages 50–3).

Extract

PROSPERO Now does my project gather to a head.
      My charms crack not, my spirits obey, and Time
      Goes upright with his carriage. How's the day?
ARIEL On the sixth hour, at which time, my lord,
      You said our work should cease.
PROSPERO   I did say so,   5
      When first I raised the tempest. Say, my spirit,
      How fares the king and's followers?
ARIEL   Confined together
      In the same fashion as you gave in charge,
      Just as you left them; all prisoners, sir,
      In the line-grove which weather-fends your cell;   10
      They cannot budge till your release. The king,
      His brother, and yours, abide all three distracted,
      And the remainder mourning over them,

Brim full of sorrow and dismay; but chiefly
Him that you termed, sir, the good old lord Gonzalo.   15
His tears runs down his beard like winter's drops
From eaves of reeds. Your charm so strongly works 'em
That if you now beheld them, your affections
Would become tender.

PROSPERO   Dost thou think so, spirit?

ARIEL   Mine would, sir, were I human.

PROSPERO   And mine shall.   20
Hast thou, which art but air, a touch, a feeling
Of their afflictions, and shall not myself,
One of their kind, that relish all as sharply
Passion as they, be kindlier moved than thou art?
Though with their high wrongs I am struck to th'quick,   25
Yet, with my nobler reason 'gainst my fury
Do I take part. The rarer action is
In virtue, than in vengeance. They being penitent,
The sole drift of my purpose doth extend
Not a frown further. Go, release them, Ariel.   30
My charms I'll break, their senses I'll restore,
And they shall be themselves.

ARIEL   I'll fetch them, sir.   *Exit*

PROSPERO   Ye elves of hills, brooks, standing lakes, and groves,
And ye that on the sands with printless foot
Do chase the ebbing Neptune, and do fly him   35
When he comes back; you demi-puppets, that
By moon-shine do the green sour ringlets make,
Whereof the ewe not bites; and you, whose pastime
Is to make midnight mushrooms, that rejoice
To hear the solemn curfew; by whose aid –   40
Weak masters though ye be – I have bedimmed
The noontide sun, called forth the mutinous winds,
And 'twixt the green sea and the azured vault
Set roaring war. To the dread rattling thunder
Have I given fire, and rifted Jove's stout oak   45
With his own bolt; the strong-based promontory
Have I made shake, and by the spurs plucked up
The pine and cedar; graves at my command
Have waked their sleepers, oped, and let 'em forth

By my so potent art. But this rough magic 50
I here abjure. And when I have required
Some heavenly music – which even now I do –
To work mine end upon their senses that
This airy charm is for, I'll break my staff,
Bury it certain fathoms in the earth, 55
And deeper than did ever plummet sound
I'll drown my book.

Example

Paragraph 1: Locate the extract in the play and identify who is on stage.
Prospero has all his enemies in his power. He feels his 'project' (plan)
is close to success: the uniting of Milan and Naples through the
marriage of Ferdinand and Miranda, and the punishment of Alonso,
Sebastian and Antonio who overthrew him as Duke of Milan. Only he
and Ariel are on stage.

Paragraph 2: State what the extract is about and identify its structure.
(Begin with one or two sentences identifying what the extract is about,
followed by several sentences briefly identifying its structure, that is,
the unfolding events and the different sections of the extract.)

The extract has three sections: Ariel's report of the madness of
Prospero's enemies; Prospero's decision to forgive; his renunciation
of his magic powers. It begins with Prospero, confident that his plan
is working, promising Ariel his freedom very shortly. Ariel tells of the
troubled state of Alonso, Sebastian and Antonio and expresses his
tender feelings for them. Prospero, profoundly affected by Ariel's
compassion for the three wrongdoers, is deeply moved and decides
on mercy. He will forgive, rather than exact vengeance. He judges his
enemies are penitent, and sends Ariel to release them so that he can
free them from their enchantment. Ariel leaves, and Prospero, alone
on stage, appeals to the spirits who have helped him to perform
awesome miracles, and declares he will give up his magic powers.

Paragraph 3: Identify the mood or atmosphere of the extract.
There are distinct shifts of mood throughout the extract. It begins with
Prospero confident, even exultant. Ariel then expresses eagerness,
longing or even resentment as he reminds Prospero of his promise to
free him. The description of the plight of Alonso and the others

conveys their suffering and Gonzalo's sorrow. Ariel's expression of pity and Prospero's response, opting for mercy, is both tender and extremely dramatic as Prospero realises, spurred by Ariel's example, the human capacity to forgive. The mood changes yet again as Prospero addresses the spirits and renounces his magical powers. It begins like a formal or religious ritual, becomes awe-inspiring in its magical claims, and ends decisively with Prospero's commitment to break his staff and drown his books.

Paragraph 4: Diction (vocabulary)

Prospero's use of 'project', an experiment carried out by an alchemist, conveys the impression of him as magician. The expressions 'gather to a head' and 'crack' also come from alchemy. *The Tempest*'s continual use of hyphenated words, helping to create the natural or mysterious qualities of the isle, occurs in 'line-grove', 'weather-fends', 'demi-puppets' and 'strong-based'. Certain key words echo themes of the play: 'Confined', 'distracted', 'virtue' and 'vengeance'. 'Virtue' has many associations: mercy, forgiveness, magnanimity, humanity, love, reason, good faith. All symbolise what Prospero recognises is involved in being human, which his 'nobler reason' requires. Prospero's description of his 'rough magic' contains vividly active expressions, 'bedimmed', 'called forth', 'Set roaring war', etc., which convey both his power and the sense of wonder that runs through the play.

Paragraph 5: Imagery

Prospero's imagery from alchemy, noted above, confirms him as a magus. He then personifies Time in an image that suggests it runs freely, conveying his confidence that everything is going his way as planned. Ariel's striking image that Gonzalo's tears fall from his beard like rain from a thatched roof calls up a picture instantly familiar to Jacobean audiences. It is introduced by the simple but telling expression 'Brim full' to describe the courtiers' sorrow. The most telling images occur as Prospero invokes his spirits, speaks of his magical powers, and then decides to give them up. Again, as all through the play, the image of the sea recurs in the ebb and flow of 'Neptune' (a personification from mythology). The images from nature of fairy rings ('green sour ringlets') and 'midnight mushrooms' add to the mysterious quality of the play, as do all the awesome images of power that follow, dimming the sun, creating tempests, thunder and lightning, and splitting mighty oaks (an image that recalls Ariel's imprisonment). Prospero's boast of his power to raise the dead creates a picture that recalls the paintings on Jacobean church walls, in which the dead rose from their graves as if awaking from sleep. Prospero's decision to renounce his magic is conveyed in clear images of simple, direct action, breaking his magic staff and burying it, and casting his books into the bottomless ocean.

Paragraph 6: Antithesis
The most striking antithesis is at the very centre of the extract, Prospero's decision that forgiveness is better than revenge: 'The rarer action is / In virtue, than in vengeance.' Some critics see this as the moral centre of the play, and the antithesis precisely conveys Prospero's choice of mercy. It is immediately preceded by antitheses that show how Prospero reached that choice. First, the contrast of Ariel's spirit nature ('but air') with Prospero's humanity ('One of their kind'), and second the opposition of his 'nobler reason' against his 'fury'. Other antitheses contribute to the effect of Prospero's renunciation speech: the ebb and flow of the tide in 'chase' and 'fly', the contrast of 'bedimmed' and 'noontide sun' and of sea and sky in 'green sea and the azured vault', and the simple but astonishing contrast of 'waked' and 'sleepers' to signify Prospero's power to revive the dead.

Paragraph 7: Repetition
There are no obvious repetitions of words and phrases, but the strongly rhythmical power of the verse is evident. That is particularly so in Prospero's final speech, which has an incantatory, ritualistic repetitiveness in its invocation to the spirits and listing of his powers. The recurring 'I' in the second half of that speech underlines both Prospero's magical power and his intention to renounce it. And in the opening exchange between Ariel and Prospero (lines 3–7), the recurrence of the 's' sound allows actors to subtly echo each other.

Paragraph 8: Lists
Shakespeare's technique of piling item on item, event on event, is most evident in his invocation to the spirits: 'Ye elves of hills, brooks, standing lakes, and groves'. That list, and what follows, conveys the vast extent of the supernatural and natural world over which Prospero exercises control. He catalogues all the miracles that his spirits and

secret studies have enabled him to perform, dimming the sun, etc. Even the final actions he decides to take ('break my staff', etc.) have an accumulating effect that adds to the impression that he will totally abandon all superhuman powers to become again simply like all other men. That intention is announced as the first item in a brief listing of how he intends to put his new-found mercy into action:

> My charms I'll break, their senses I'll restore,
> And they shall be themselves.   *(lines 31–2)*

Paragraph 9: Staging opportunities

The extract offers opportunities to show aspects of the relationship between Prospero and Ariel, and of Prospero's complex character. For example, Ariel's first two lines can be used to hint at his resentment in having so long served Prospero, and his eagerness for freedom. Prospero's response 'I did say so', may be curtly or kindly spoken. This brief exchange enables actors to show their interpretation of the master–servant relationship. But the most dramatic opportunity for showing their relationship occurs at the centre of the extract as Prospero learns compassion and forgiveness from his spirit attendant. Prospero's 'Dost thou think so, spirit?' can be an amazed dawning of realisation of Ariel's compassion for the troubled wrongdoers. Prompted by Ariel's words, Prospero's opting for mercy, 'And mine shall', can be a supremely theatrical moment, a moving experience for the audience, as Prospero struggles with his emotions, then finally pities his enemies and decides to forgive them. However it is performed, it should be a memorable moment for the audience, because it marks a crucial moral shift in Prospero's character. In Prospero's long speech that then follows it is customary for him to move centre stage, and in vocally commanding tones call up his spirits and catalogue his mighty powers. But the final lines as he renounces his powers demand a change of tone. He is still utterly determined, but no longer authoritarian or boastful. At the lines 'But this rough magic / I here abjure', the actor usually changes from the impression of an all-powerful magus to the quiet determination of a mortal man.

Paragraph 10: Conclusion

The extract vividly conveys the changes that Prospero undergoes, from revenger to forgiver, from magician to man. As such it powerfully conveys the play's theme of the desire for vengeance changing to a preference for mercy and reconciliation. It also expresses many of the other themes or preoccupations of the play: magic, confinement and release, the sea, wonder and enchantment, and, in the 'heavenly music' that Prospero calls for to release his enemies from their enchantment, the ever-changing music that runs through the play.

Reminders

- The framework is only a guide. It helps you to structure your writing. Use the framework for practice on other extracts. Adapt as you feel appropriate. Make it your own.
- Structure your response in paragraphs. Each paragraph makes a particular point and helps build up your argument.
- Focus tightly on the language, especially vocabulary, imagery, antithesis, lists, repetition.
- Remember that *The Tempest* is a play, a drama intended for performance. The purpose of writing about an extract is to identify how Shakespeare creates dramatic effect. What techniques does he use?
- Try to imagine the action. Visualise the scene in your mind's eye. But remember there can be many valid ways of performing a scene. Offer alternatives. Justify your own preferences by reference to the language.
- Who is on stage? Imagine their interaction. How do 'silent characters' react to what is said?
- Look for the theatrical qualities of the extract. What guides for actors' movement and expressions are given in the language? Comment on any stage directions.
- How might the audience respond? In Jacobean times? Today? How might you respond as a member of the audience?
- How might the lines be spoken? Think about tone, emphasis, pace, pauses. Identify shifting moods and registers. Is the verse pattern smooth or broken, flowing or full of hesitations and abrupt turns?
- What is the importance of the extract in the play as a whole? Justify its thematic significance.
- Are there 'key words'?

- Try to find examples of Shakespeare's 'late plays' style: compression, hyphenated words, awkward syntax.
- How does the extract develop the plot, reveal character, deepen themes?
- Offer a variety of interpretations.

Writing an essay

As part of your study of *The Tempest* you will be asked to write essays, either under examination conditions or for coursework (term papers). Examinations mean that you are under pressure of time, usually having around one hour to prepare and write each essay. Coursework means that you have much longer to think about and produce your essay. But whatever the type of essay, each will require you to develop an argument about a particular aspect of *The Tempest*.

Before suggesting a strategy for your essay-writing, it is helpful to recall just what an essay is. Essay comes from the French *essayer*: to attempt, or to make a trial. It was originally used by the sixteenth-century French writer Montaigne (whose work Shakespeare certainly read, see page 68). Montaigne used *essais* to attempt to find out what he thought about particular subjects, such as 'friendship' or 'cannibals' or 'education'. In each essay he used many practical examples to test his response to the topic.

The essays you write on *The Tempest* similarly require that you set out your thoughts on a particular aspect of the play, using evidence from the text. The people who read your essays (examiners, teachers, lecturers) will have certain expectations of your writing. In each essay they will expect you to discuss and analyse a particular topic, using evidence from the play to develop an argument in an organised, coherent and persuasive way. Examiners look for, and reward, what they call 'an informed personal response'. This simply means that you show you have good knowledge of the play ('informed') and can use evidence from it to support and justify your own viewpoint ('personal').

You can write about *The Tempest* from different points of view. As pages 93–106 show, you can approach the play from a number of critical perspectives (postcolonial, feminist, political, psychoanalytic, etc.). You can also set the play in its social, literary, political and other contexts, as shown in the Contexts section (pages 64–78). You should write at different levels, moving beyond description to analysis and evaluation. Simply telling the story or describing characters is not as effective as analysing how events or characters embody wider concerns of the play. In *The Tempest*, these 'wider concerns' (also called themes, issues, preoccupations – or more simply 'what the play is about') are listed on page 93. In your writing, always give practical examples (quotations, actions) that illustrate the themes you discuss.

How should you answer an examination question or write a coursework essay? The following three-fold structure can help you organise your response:

opening paragraph
developing paragraphs
concluding paragraph.

Opening paragraph Begin with a paragraph identifying just what topic or issue you will focus on. Show that you have understood what the question is about. You probably will have prepared for particular topics. But look closely at the question and identify key words to see what particular aspect it asks you to write about. Adapt your material to answer that question. Examiners do not reward an essay, however well-written, if it is not on the question set.

Developing paragraphs This is the main body of your essay. In it you develop your argument, point by point, paragraph by paragraph. Use evidence from the play that illuminates the topic or issue, and answers the question set. Each paragraph makes a point of dramatic or thematic significance. Some paragraphs could make points concerned with context or particular critical approaches. The effect of your argument builds up as each paragraph adds to the persuasive quality of your essay. Use brief quotations that support your argument, and show clearly just why they are relevant. Ensure that your essay demonstrates that you are aware that *The Tempest* is a play, a drama intended for performance, and therefore open to a wide variety of interpretations and audience response.

Concluding paragraph Your final paragraph pulls together your main conclusions. It does not simply repeat what you have written earlier, but summarises concisely how your essay has successfully answered the question.

Example

Question: How far do you agree with the claim that 'to understand Prospero is to understand *The Tempest*'?

The following notes show the 'ingredients' of an answer. In an examination it is usually helpful to prepare similar notes from which you write your essay, paragraph by paragraph. To help you understand how contextual matters or points from different critical approaches might be included, the words 'Context' or 'Criticism' appear before some items. Remember that examiners are not impressed by 'name-dropping': use of critics' names. What they want you to show is your knowledge and judgement of the play and its contexts, and of how it has been interpreted from different critical perspectives.

Opening paragraph
Show you are aware that the question asks you to give your own judgement on the statement. Remember that all such quotations are arguable, so your task is to provide evidence supporting the quotation and evidence that contests it and, on consideration of both evidence 'for' and 'against', to give your own view. So include the following points and aim to write a sentence or more on each:

- The statement seems to imply that Prospero's viewpoint provides the key to understanding the play.
- Criticism But interpretations of Prospero, and of *The Tempest*, have changed radically over time.
- Other characters' viewpoints need to be taken into account to gain a more comprehensive understanding of the play. Shakespeare always provides many such viewpoints.
- It is necessary to show some of the major ways in which Prospero has been understood and to judge how far each might represent an understanding of *The Tempest* (what the play is about).

Following paragraphs

Now write a paragraph on each of a number of different ways in which Prospero has been interpreted, and in each suggest how that might or might not represent important aspects of the play (dramatic, thematic, etc.), confirming or questioning the statement. Some of the points you might include are given briefly below.

- *Benign or malignant?* Criticism: performance Prospero was traditionally portrayed as a benign old man who wished to restore harmony and achieve reconciliation. But in modern criticism and productions he has been portrayed as deeply troubled, harsh and demanding. The conception of the whole play has similarly changed from a harmless fairytale to an ambiguous, socially critical drama (e.g. as a critique of colonialism).

- *Magician* Context Prospero is a magus and scholar who learned to practise magic. His books and his spirits enable him to control the natural world. But the play shows he finds it difficult to control human nature, other people's and his own.

- *Slave owner and master* Context and criticism: political and postcolonial Prospero controls Caliban harshly with cramps and pinches. He also exercises stern control over Ariel with mingled affection and irritation, using a blend of praise and threats. The play is much concerned with imprisonment and freedom, but a more complete understanding of this issue comes from considering Caliban's and Ariel's viewpoints ('This island's mine').

- *Prince* Criticism: political Prospero's self centred pursuit of study made him neglect his civic duties, and led to his overthrow as Duke of Milan. Much of the play reflects similar political struggle for power: Sebastian's murderous desire to become King of Naples, Stephano's attempt to become ruler of the island.

- *Father* Criticism: feminist and political Prospero plans that his daughter should marry the man of his choice, Ferdinand, and so achieve the union of Milan and Naples. But his obsession with sexual purity and political reconciliation is challenged by other aspects of the play (Caliban's and Stephano's desire for Miranda, Antonio's ominous silence at the end).

- *Revenger* Criticism: traditional It seems Prospero seeks revenge on Alonso, Antonio and Sebastian for bringing about his overthrow and banishment. But, moved by Ariel's pity for their plight, he pardons them. This suggests the play is about mercy ('The rarer action is / In virtue, than in vengeance'). But it is possible he intended forgiveness from the start (because he prevents the murder of Alonso).

- *Actor-manager* Criticism: performance Prospero is like a theatre director. He stages the opening tempest; he ensures that Alonso and Gonzalo sleep, so provoking the murder attempt by Antonio and Sebastian; he is the unseen observer of his daughter and his enemies; and he produces the banquet and the masque. The play is full of 'theatrical' language and allusions, but Prospero, like the other characters he 'directs', is a character in a play.

- *Man* Criticism: traditional The play can be read as showing Prospero's development from powerful magician and potential revenger to a vulnerable and merciful human being. Almost at the end of the play, Prospero renounces all his magical powers. In the Epilogue he admits to his weakness, 'Now my charms are all o'erthrown, / And what strength I have's mine own'. But the play is about much more than Prospero's transformation. Other characters reveal very different aspects of human personality, behaviour and desires.

- *Name* Prospero's name derives from Latin words meaning 'fortunate' or 'prosperous'. But the outcome of his 'project' is only partially successful. Antonio and Sebastian seem unrepentant at the play's end.

- *Shakespeare* Context and criticism: traditional Many critics have argued that Shakespeare wrote the part of Prospero as a self-portrait, particularly in his 'Our revels now are ended' speech and in the renunciation of his magic art. But most critics see this as fanciful, unprovable speculation.

Concluding paragraph
Write several sentences pulling together your conclusions. You might include the following points:

- There is a strong sense in which Prospero's words and actions express major aspects of the play, as shown above.

- Context and criticism But to take only his perspective on aspects such as usurpation, colonialism, forgiveness and reconciliation, justice and mercy, imprisonment and freedom, is to limit more complete understanding of these key themes in the play.

- Context and criticism To give only three examples, *The Tempest* should be understood by taking into account Gonzalo's commonwealth, Caliban's resentment and claim to the island, and the strange nature of Ariel and his longing for freedom.

- Criticism: performance Over four centuries, changing interpretations of both Prospero and the play have demonstrated that an understanding of *The Tempest* involves more than a consideration of Prospero alone.

Writing about character

As the Critical approaches section showed (pages 88–106), much critical writing about *The Tempest* traditionally focused on characters, writing about them as if they were living human beings. Today it is not sufficient just to describe their personalities. When you write about characters you will also be expected to show that they are dramatic constructs, part of Shakespeare's stagecraft. They embody the wider concerns of the play, have certain dramatic functions, and are set in a social and political world with particular values and beliefs. They reflect and express issues of significance to Shakespeare's society – and today's.

Everything you read in this Guide is written with those principles in mind, and can be a model for your own writing. Of course you should say what a character seems like to you, but you should also write about how Shakespeare makes him or her part of his overall dramatic design. For example Shakespeare creates dramatic patterns by making characters equivalent or contrasting in their dramatic functions:

- Prospero and his 'white magic' contrasts with Sycorax and 'black magic'.
- Just as Antonio usurps Prospero as Duke of Milan, so Prospero usurps Caliban as owner of the island.
- Caliban's earthiness contrasts with Ariel as a spirit of air.
- Ferdinand and Miranda can be seen as stock figures of romance: noble prince and pure maiden.
- Gonzalo's integrity and sincerity is contrasted with Sebastian's and Antonio's perfidy and cynicism.

- Stephano and Trinculo are the drunken, comic equivalents of Sebastian and Antonio in their wish to achieve power through murder.

But there is a danger in writing about the functions of characters or the character types they represent. Prospero, for example, is much more than the traditional usurped prince or powerful magician. Actors can portray him as a believable deeply troubled human being, complex and contradictory. To reduce a character to a mere plot device is just as inappropriate as treating them as a real person. Shakespeare gives even minor characters the opportunity to make a significant impression on the audience as recognisable human beings.

When you write about characters in *The Tempest*, you should try to achieve a balance between analysing their personality, identifying the dilemmas they face and placing them in their social, critical and dramatic contexts. That style of writing is found all through this Guide, and that, together with the following brief discussions of four characters, can help inform your own written responses.

Prospero

Prospero is discussed in some detail throughout the commentary (pages 5–63) and on pages 118–21. Here, only a few more points are made. The critic Dover Wilson saw him as 'a terrible old man, almost as tyrannical and irascible as Lear at the opening of his play'. In striking contrast, the modern critic R S White compares him to a modern computer buff, 'manipulating his little world with the expertise of somebody playing a series of interactive media games'. Merely to list some of the ways Prospero has been interpreted is to understand the complex and contradictory character Shakespeare has created: 'noble ruler', 'tyrant', 'megalomaniac', 'colonialist', 'necromancer' (dealing in black magic), 'neoplatonic scientist' (an experimenter who uses 'magic' for good purposes), 'an exiled, embittered, manipulative wizard', 'a benevolent, god-like, justified ruler of the island', 'obsessed with control'.

Prospero was traditionally portrayed as a well-intentioned magician, a serene old man whose 'project' was to restore harmony and achieve reconciliation. But in many twentieth-century productions he was played as a much more ambiguous figure, harsh, demanding and impatient. Prospero uses his magic to cause other characters to fear and wonder. For a long time he believed his purpose was to master nature through magical studies. However, he comes to see that to be truly human is to be merciful.

Ariel

Ariel is described in the list of characters as 'an airy spirit', and has been played by both male and female actors. As the play progresses Ariel appears in different guises: a flaming light in the storm, a nymph of the sea, a harpy at the banquet, Ceres in the masque. At Prospero's command, Ariel performs near-impossible feats such as fetching 'dew from the still-vexed Bermudas', treading 'the ooze of the salt deep' and running 'upon the sharp wind of the north'.

Imprisoned by Sycorax for refusing to obey her orders, and freed by Prospero's magic, only to have to serve him, Ariel yearns for freedom throughout the play. Prospero's attitude to his spirit-servant is ambiguous. Sometimes he seems affectionate, calling Ariel 'bird', 'chick', 'my fine spirit'. But at other times he calls Ariel 'moody' or 'malignant thing'. When Ariel demands his liberty, Prospero threatens him with 12 more years of imprisonment.

Ariel's language often expresses rapid movement and breathless excitement. There is a child-like eagerness to please in 'What shall I do? / Say what? What shall I do?' It is Ariel who teaches Prospero compassion and forgiveness (but it should be noted that many critics claim that Prospero intended mercy from the start).

Caliban

Caliban seems to embody Jacobean fantasies of 'the savage': deformed, lustful, treacherous and rebellious, drunken, and easily swayed to worship new gods. In the list of characters he is described as 'a savage and deformed slave', and in all kinds of uncomplimentary ways in the play itself: 'filth', 'hag-seed', 'misshapen knave'. Stephano and Trinculo continually call him 'monster' ('shallow monster', 'howling monster', and so on). On stage he has been played as a lizard, a dog, a monkey, a snake and a fish. Every production faces the problem of how to present him, and the responses have ranged from bizarre animality to a fully human being.

In the eighteenth century, the comic aspects of the role were emphasised. Caliban was a figure of fun, not to be taken seriously. In recent times, performances have emphasised Caliban's human and tragic qualities, not just his wickedness. He has increasingly been seen as a native dispossessed of his language and land by a colonial exploiter (see pages 96–9). The following brief notes identify different critical approaches to Caliban's character:

Victim A ruthless exploiter takes over Caliban's island, forcing him into slavery. He is viewed by callous Europeans as an opportunity to make money.

Savage Caliban is brutish and evil by nature, incapable of being educated or civilised ('on whose nature / Nurture can never stick'). His plot against Prospero reflects his violent and vindictive nature, and he had tried to rape Miranda.

Servant Caliban deserves to be a slave. He merely exchanges a harsh master (Prospero) for a drunken one (Stephano). He believes Stephano to be a god and wants to serve him as his 'foot-licker'.

Contrast Caliban's function in the play is to act as a contrast to other characters, for example as lust versus pure love (Ferdinand), and natural malevolence versus 'civilised' evil (Antonio).

Noble savage Until Prospero arrived, Caliban lived in natural freedom. He loves the island, and his language eloquently expresses its wonders. He speaks some of the most haunting verse in the play when he responds to Ariel's music that so frightens his co-conspirators, 'Be not afeared, the isle is full of noises'.

Symbol of wickedness Many of Shakespeare's contemporaries wrongly believed that physical deformity was a sign of the wickedness of the parents. Prospero claims that Caliban is the son of a witch and the Devil.

Miranda

Miranda's role seems to be that of dutiful daughter and future wife, pure and innocent. She falls in love at first sight with the prince her father plans to be her husband. As such she seems little more than the stereotypical maiden of romance. But Shakespeare complicates her character. She tries to stand up for Ferdinand against her father; she secretly meets Ferdinand, and in telling him her name disobeys Prospero's command; and she directs what seems an uncharacteristic torrent of abuse at Caliban (see page 13).

Resources

Books

Francis Barker and **Peter Hulme**, 'Nymphs and Reapers Heavily Vanish: The Discursive Con-texts of *The Tempest*', in R S White (ed.), *The Tempest: New Casebooks*, Macmillan, 1999
An essay that uses poststructuralist concepts, but which can be read as postcolonial criticism in its view that traditional criticism of *The Tempest* has been complicit with colonialist ideology.

Philip Brockbank (ed.), *Players of Shakespeare 1*, Cambridge University Press, 1985
Contains a fascinating account by actor David Suchet of his approach to the role of Caliban.

Dympna Callaghan, *Shakespeare without Women*, Routledge, 1999
The chapter 'Irish memories in *The Tempest*' argues that the play reflects many of the oppressive features that characterise the English colonisation of Ireland.

Christine Dymkowski (ed.), *The Tempest: Shakespeare in Production*, Cambridge University Press, 2000
An account of the stage history of *The Tempest* in Britain and America, together with productions in other countries. Excellent for developing an understanding of the changing meanings of the play in different times and cultures.

Stephen Greenblatt, *Shakespearean Negotiations: The Circulation of Social Energy in Renaissance England*, University of California Press, 1988
A 'New Historicist' approach to the plays which relates them to the political and cultural contexts of Shakespeare's time. Examines *The Tempest* through consideration of the 1610 Strachey letter detailing rebellions against the governor of Virginia.

Frank Kermode, *Shakespeare's Language*, Allen Lane, Penguin, 2000   p.
A detailed examination of how Shakespeare's language changed over the course of his playwriting career. Contains a helpful section on *The Tempest*.

Frank Kermode, 'Introduction to *The Tempest*', in D J Palmer (ed.), *Shakespeare: The Tempest, A Casebook*, Macmillan, 1968   p. 151 – 167
A highly regarded essay that interprets *The Tempest* as a pastoral play with the opposition of Art and Nature as its central theme.

G Wilson Knight, 'The Shakespearean Superman', in D J Palmer (ed.), *Shakespeare: The Tempest, A Casebook*, Macmillan, 1968   p. 111 – 131
Published first in 1947, Knight's chapter considers *The Tempest* in the context of all Shakespeare's plays to detect similarities and parallels in characters, themes and

actions. He argues that Prospero embodies features of many other major Shakespearean characters.

Jan Kott, *Shakespeare Our Contemporary*, Methuen, 1965
An influential political reading of Shakespeare's plays. The chapter 'Prospero's Staff' is reprinted in D J Palmer (ed.), *Shakespeare: The Tempest, A Casebook*, Macmillan, 1968.

Douglas Lanier, 'Drowning the Book: Prospero's Books and the Textual Shakespeare', in Robert Shaughnessy (ed.), *Shakespeare on Film: New Casebooks*, Macmillan, 1998
A postmodern essay which interprets Peter Greenaway's film (see below) as a radical questioning of the authority of Shakespeare's text.

Ania Loomba, 'Seizing the Book', in R S White (ed.), *The Tempest: New Casebooks*, Macmillan, 1999
An important essay that conveys a clear account of major features of postcolonial approaches to the play. Shows how such approaches involve issues of race, ethnicity, gender and class.

Ruth Nevo, 'Subtleties of the Isle: *The Tempest*', in R S White (ed.), *The Tempest: New Casebooks*, Macmillan, 1999
A psychoanalytic approach that argues *The Tempest* is 'Shakespeare's most indissolubly tragi-comic drama'.

D J Palmer (ed.), *Shakespeare: The Tempest, A Casebook*, Macmillan, 1968
Contains a valuable collection of critical writing on the play from 1679 to 1964 including criticism by Kermode, Knight, Kott, Tillyard and Zimbardo noted in this booklist.

Shakespeare Survey 43 'The Tempest and After', Cambridge University Press, 1990
Available in or through college libraries. This issue of an annual journal which surveys Shakespeare studies and Shakespeare productions concentrates on *The Tempest*.

Robert Shaughnessy (ed.), *Shakespeare on Film: New Casebooks*, Macmillan, 1998
Colin MacCabe's provocative essay on Derek Jarman's *The Tempest* and Douglas Lanier's similarly radical appreciation of Peter Greenaway's *Prospero's Books* are thought-provoking readings which challenge traditional understandings of Shakespeare.

Nigel Smith, 'The Italian Job: Magic and Machiavelli in *The Tempest*', in Linda Cookson and Bryan Loughrey (eds.), *Critical Essays on The Tempest*, Longman, 1988
An account of the play in terms of Shakespeare's familiarity with politics in courts and states of Renaissance Italy, together with his reading of Machiavelli's *The Prince*. Other essays in this collection deserve attention as they were especially written for a student readership.

Caroline Spurgeon, *Shakespeare's Imagery and What It Tells Us*, Cambridge University Press, 1935
The first major study of imagery in the plays. Although much criticised today, Spurgeon's identification of image-clusters as a dominant feature of the plays has influenced later studies.

Ann Thompson, '"Miranda, Where's Your Sister?" Reading Shakespeare's *The Tempest*', in R S White (ed.), *The Tempest: New Casebooks*, Macmillan, 1999
Thompson gives an outline of a possible feminist approach to the play, noting its 'obsession with themes of chastity and fertility' and how those themes are expressed in terms of male control.

E M W Tillyard, 'The Tragic Pattern', in D J Palmer (ed.), *Shakespeare: The Tempest, A Casebook*, Macmillan, 1968
First published in 1954, Tillyard's chapter detects tragedy in the story Prospero tells of his deposition, but argues that he is inclined to mercy, not revenge, from the very start of the play.

Alden T Vaughan and **Virginia Mason Vaughan**, *Shakespeare's Caliban: A Cultural History*, Cambridge University Press, 1991
Traces how Caliban over the centuries has been represented on stage in ways that range from monstrous savage to colonial victim.

R S White (ed.), *The Tempest: New Casebooks*, Macmillan, 1999
A valuable collection of modern criticism: political, feminist, psychoanalytic and post-structuralist. Contains extracts from or essays by Barker and Hulme, Loomba, and Thompson mentioned in this booklist. White's introduction is fresh and thought-provoking, for example in conceiving Prospero's 'art' as analogous to the computer: the shipwreck is an anticipation of virtual reality in which the survivors' clothes can be miraculously cleaned 'just as one can control and tidy a messy screen or document with a touch of the "Clean Up desktop" button'.

Rose Abdelnour Zimbardo, 'Form and Disorder in *The Tempest*', in D J Palmer (ed.), *Shakespeare: The Tempest, A Casebook*, Macmillan, 1968
Zimbardo rejects the critical assumption that the play is about regeneration, and interprets it instead in terms of the opposition between order and chaos.

Films

The Tempest (UK, 1979) Director: John Gorrie
Made for the BBC television series of all Shakespeare's plays. Michael Horden's Prospero was judged 'dignified but undisturbing'.

The Tempest (UK, 1979) Director: Derek Jarman
Neglects political aspects of the play to focus on homoerotic relationships. Set in a decaying mansion where Prospero uses Ariel as a spy. Caliban is white. Miranda displays compulsive sexuality. The film ends with the wedding masque becoming

a sailors' dance, as if from a gay cabaret, and with a spirited singing of 'Stormy Weather' by Elizabeth Welch. One critic described the film as 'nostalgic flower-power escapism'.

The Tempest (UK, 1992)
A half-hour animated version, adapted by Leon Garfield, available in the Animated Tales series.

The characters and plot of *The Tempest* have also provided the inspiration for a number of screen adaptations. These include:

Yellow Sky (USA, 1948) Director: William Wellman
An old prospector and his granddaughter live in a desert ghost town. A band of outlaws arrive, and the town, like Prospero's island, becomes a place where true character is revealed.

Forbidden Planet (USA, 1956) Director: Fred McLeod Wilcox
A science fiction film set in 2257. Ariel becomes Robby the Robot, Prospero is Dr Morbius, and Caliban is Dr Morbius' unconscious ('this thing of darkness, I / Acknowledge mine'). The film, made during the cold war between Soviet and capitalist countries, reflects contemporary anxieties about scientists' responsibilities (especially concerning the development of nuclear weapons).

Prospero's Books (UK, 1991) Director: Peter Greenaway
A postmodern adaptation in which John Gielgud plays Prospero (looking like the Doge of Venice), who writes and speaks almost all the other characters' lines. Nudity, bodily movement and functions are emphatically and grotesquely emphasised. Ariel urinates on a model boat to conjure up the opening tempest, and Caliban variously excretes and vomits on Prospero's books. Interpreted by Douglas Lanier (see booklist) as 'a series of static though visually sumptuous dumb shows that emblematise the text's imagery', and as 'postmodern bricolage', which some sceptical viewers might interpret as 'confusing rubbish'.

Audio books
Four major versions are easily available, in the series produced by Naxos, Arkangel, HarperCollins and the BBC Radio Collection.

The Tempest on the Web
If you type 'Shakespeare The Tempest' into your search engine, it will find over 100,000 items. Because websites are of wildly varying quality, and rapidly disappear or are created, no recommendation can safely be made. But if you have time to browse, you may find much of interest.